Best-Loved
Slow Cooker Recipes

pi

Publications International, Ltd.

Pictured on front cover: Three-Bean Mole Chili *(page 140)*.

Pictured on back cover: Wild Mushroom Beef Stew *(page 69)*, Scalloped Potatoes and Ham *(page 70)*, Chicken Tortilla Soup *(page 104)*, Cioppino *(page 108)*.

Photography on pages 11, 13, 15, 21, 29, 33, 49, 53, 67, 77, 86, 91, 97, 101, 103, 113, 117, 129, 133, 139, 145, 149, 157, 161, 163, 171, 183, 184, 185, 201, 203, 205, 213, 215, 219, 231, 235, 239 and 245 by Stephen Hamilton Photographics, Chicago.

Photographers: Tate Hunt, Eric Coughlin
Photographers' assistant: Christy Clow
Prop stylist: Tom Hamilton
Food stylists: Kim Hartman, Rick Longhi, Mary Helen Steindler
Assistant food stylists: Constance Pikulas, Christina Zerkis

ISBN 13: 978-1-4127-2497-5
ISBN 10: 1-4127-2497-X

Manufactured in China.

8 7 6 5 4 3 2 1

Table of Contents

CROCK-POT® Slow Cooker

Basics

This fast guide to slow cooking will enhance your experience and your results. Additional helpful tips can be found throughout the chapters.

Slow Cooker Capacity

In general, **CROCK-POT®** slow cooker recipes are developed for the medium-size slow cooker, or one that accommodates 3½ to 4 quarts. But **CROCK-POT®** slow cookers do come in a lot of sizes, and range from as small as 1 quart to as large as 7 quarts. Usually, the smaller sizes are deep and narrow, while the larger sizes are wider and rounder.

If you're not sure what size your **CROCK-POT®** slow cooker is, there's a simple way to check its capacity. Just fill a measuring cup with 8 ounces of water. Pour it into the stoneware, then keep track of how many cups it takes to fill the stoneware to the rim. Remember, 2 cups equal 1 pint, and 4 cups equal 1 quart. If your slow cooker holds 3½ to 4 quarts, you should get 14 to 16 cups of water into it, and so on.

Cooking Temperatures and Food Safety

Cooking meats in your **CROCK-POT®** slow cooker is perfectly safe. According to the U.S. Department of Agriculture, bacteria in food is killed at a temperature in excess of 170°F for beef and as high as 209°F for poultry. However, to reach these temperatures, it's important to follow the recommended cooking times and to keep the cover on your **CROCK-POT®** slow cooker during the cooking process. At the end of the cooking time, check the internal temperatures of poultry and meat using an instant-read thermometer. Poultry should be at least 180°F, and beef and pork should be 160°F to 170°F.

If your food isn't done after 8 hours when the recipe calls for 8 to 10 hours, this could be due to voltage variations, which are commonplace; to altitude; or even to extreme humidity. Slight fluctuations in power don't have a noticeable effect on most appliances; however, they can slightly alter the cooking times. Allow your food to continue cooking until it's done.

If you arrive home and find the electrical power service to your home is out, check the **CROCK-POT**® slow cooker immediately. With an instant-read thermometer, check the internal temperature of the contents in the **CROCK-POT**® slow cooker. If the temperature is above 140°F, you can transfer the contents to a large saucepan or Dutch oven and finish cooking it on a gas range or gas grill. However, if the temperature of the food is between 40°F and 140°F—the "danger zone" temperatures at which bacteria thrive—throw the food away.

If the electricity is on when you arrive home, but you can tell by the clocks that your home has been without power, the best thing to do is throw away the food. You'll never know what the temperature of the food was when the power went off or how long it was off; the food may have spent several hours in the danger zone. And, although the food is hot when you get home and looks done, it's better to err on the side of safety and throw it away.

Allow plenty of time, and remember: It's practically impossible to overcook food in a **CROCK-POT**® slow cooker. You'll learn through experience whether to decrease or increase cooking times.

Stirring

Due to the nature of slow cooking, there's no need to stir the food unless it specifically says to in your recipe. In fact, taking the lid off to stir food can cause a **CROCK-POT**® slow cooker to lose a significant amount of heat, extending the cooking time required. It can take as long as 30 minutes to regain the heat lost when the lid is removed during cooking. So, it's best not to remove the lid for stirring.

If you can't resist the urge to peek, just tap the lid gently or spin it lightly to remove some of the condensation and see what's going on inside.

Removable Stoneware

The removable stoneware in your **CROCK-POT**® slow cooker makes cleaning easy. Here are some tips on the use and care of your stoneware:

When cooking sticky foods, such as barbecued ribs, desserts, or other dishes that contain sugary ingredients, coat the stoneware with nonstick cooking spray for easier cleanup. To remove any sticky food, soak the stoneware in hot sudsy water, then scrub with a plastic or nylon scrubber. *Don't use steel wool.*

Don't preheat the **CROCK-POT**® slow cooker.

Because all **CROCK-POT**® slow cookers have wrap-around heat, there's no direct heat from the bottom. For best results, always fill the stoneware at least half full to conform to recommended times. Small quantities can still be cooked, but cooking times will be affected.

The stoneware insert can be damaged by sudden changes in temperature. Don't place a cold insert into a preheated base. Don't place a hot insert on a cold surface or in the refrigerator; don't fill it with cold water. Don't place a cold insert in a conventional or microwave oven. Never place stoneware in the freezer.

Don't use the stoneware insert if it's cracked; replace it. For further safety tips, refer to the instruction manual that came with your **CROCK-POT**® slow cooker.

Your **CROCK-POT**® slow cooker makes a great server for hot beverages, appetizers, or dips. Keep it on the WARM setting to maintain the proper serving temperature.

Browning Meat

Meat cooked in the **CROCK-POT**® slow cooker won't brown as it would if cooked in a skillet or oven at high temperatures. For some recipes, it's not necessary to brown the meat. But, if you prefer the look and flavor of browned meat, brown the meat in a skillet before placing it in the stoneware; follow the recipe as written.

Adding Ingredients at the End of the Cooking Time

Certain ingredients tend to break down during extended cooking. When possible, add these ingredients toward the end of the cooking time:

Milk, cream, and sour cream: Add during the last 15 minutes of cooking time.

Seafood: Add in the last 3 to 15 minutes, depending on the thickness and quantity. Gently stir periodically to ensure even cooking.

Vegetables: Long cooking can cause vegetables to lose their bright color. To avoid this problem, add delicate vegetables near the end of cooking.

Cooking for Larger Quantity Yields

If you want to prepare recipes in a larger unit, such as a 5-, 6-, or 7-quart **CROCK-POT**® slow cooker, follow these guidelines when recipes don't specifically call for the larger unit:

Roasted meat, chicken, and turkey quantities may be doubled or tripled, but seasonings should be adjusted by no more than half. Flavorful seasonings, such as garlic and chili powder, intensify during long, slow cooking. Add just 25 to 50 percent more spices, as needed to balance flavors.

When preparing a soup or a stew, you may double all ingredients except seasonings (see above), dried herbs, liquids, and thickeners. Increase liquid volume by no more than half, or as needed. The **CROCK-POT**® slow cooker lid collects steam, which condenses to keep foods moist and to maintain liquid volume. Do not double thickeners, such as cornstarch, at the beginning. You may always add more thickener later if needed.

When preparing dishes with beef or pork in a larger unit, such as a 5-, 6-, or 7-quart **CROCK-POT**® slow cooker, browning the meat in a skillet before adding it to the stoneware yields the best results; the meat will cook more evenly.

When preparing baked goods, it's best not to double or triple the recipe. Just prepare the original recipe as many times as needed to serve more people.

High-Altitude Adjustments

If you live at an altitude above 3,500 feet, you'll need to make some adjustments when slow cooking. Everything takes longer to cook, so plan for that. Tough meats take longer to tenderize at high altitudes—sometimes much longer. Try cooking meat on the HIGH heat setting instead of LOW. Root vegetables also take longer to cook; for quicker cooking, cut smaller pieces than a recipe suggests.

Recipes provide a range of cooking times to account for variables, such as the temperature of the ingredients before cooking and the quantity of food in your **CROCK-POT**® slow cooker, as well as the altitude. Just keep in mind that the suggested cooking times are guidelines. Always use an instant-read thermometer to confirm your dishes are done.

CROCK-POT® Slow Cooker

Techniques

for Special Foods

Frozen Foods

Although you may cook frozen foods in a **CROCK-POT**® slow cooker, it's best to avoid doing so. Instead, thaw frozen meat in the refrigerator before cooking. If you must use frozen meat, add at least 1 cup of warm or hot liquid to the stoneware before adding the frozen meat; don't preheat the unit. Remember to add more cooking time, and check the finished dish with an instant-read thermometer to make sure the meat has reached a safe internal temperature.

It's best not to cook packages of frozen vegetables in a **CROCK-POT**® slow cooker; instead, thaw them or cook them on the stove top or in a microwave oven. You may add small amounts (½ to 1 cup) of frozen vegetables, such as peas, corn, green beans, and broccoli florets, to a slow-cooked meal during the last 30 to 45 minutes of cooking. Cook on the HIGH setting until the vegetables are tender. (You may need to add a few minutes to the cooking time.)

Rice

Choose converted long-grain rice (or Arborio rice when suggested) or wild rice for best results. Long, slow cooking can turn other types of rice into mush; if you prefer to use other types of rice instead of converted rice, cook them conventionally and add them to the **CROCK-POT**® slow cooker during the last 15 minutes of cooking.

You can add a small amount (½ cup) of uncooked rice to a **CROCK-POT**® slow cooker soup or other dish; be sure to add it to boiling liquid during the last hour of cooking and cook on the HIGH setting. If it doesn't seem completely cooked after the suggested time, you may add an extra ½ to 1 cup of liquid per cup of rice, and extend the cooking time by 30 to 60 minutes.

Pasta

Pasta needs to be cooked in a large quantity of boiling water; it should not be cooked in a **CROCK-POT**® slow cooker. However, you can add small amounts (½ to 1 cup) of small pasta, such as orzo, small shell macaroni, ditali, and short lengths of linguine, to boiling liquid during the last hour of slow cooking. You may also cook pasta in boiling water and add it to the **CROCK-POT**® slow cooker during the last 30 minutes of cooking.

Fish

Fish cooks quickly and easily overcooks. Choose only firm white fish, such as cod, haddock, sea bass, red snapper, or orange roughy. Avoid more delicate varieties and thin fillets because they'll fall apart. Thaw frozen fish overnight in its original packaging before cooking it.

Add the fish 30 to 45 minutes before the end of the cooking time. Change the heat setting to HIGH before you add the fish, cover the **CROCK-POT**® slow cooker and cook until the fish just begins to flake when tested with a fork. The cooking time depends on the quantity and the thickness of the fillets—the thicker the fillets and the more of them, the longer they take to cook.

Shellfish

Shellfish, such as shrimp, are delicate and should be added to the **CROCK-POT**® slow cooker during the last 15 to 30 minutes of cooking time. Always use a HIGH heat setting for shellfish. If you add a large quantity of shellfish to the **CROCK-POT**® slow cooker, you may need to add a little extra cooking time. Watch shellfish carefully; it overcooks easily.

Dried Beans

Presoak dried beans before cooking them in a **CROCK-POT**® slow cooker. This softens them and gives them a head start on cooking. (Lentils and split peas do not need to be presoaked.) There are two methods for presoaking:

Traditional method: Place sorted and rinsed dried beans in a bowl. Cover them with cold, unsalted water and let them stand overnight. Drain off the water and place the beans in the **CROCK-POT**® slow cooker.

Quick method: Place sorted and rinsed beans in a large saucepan; cover them with twice their volume of cold unsalted water. Bring the water to a boil over high heat. Boil for 2 minutes. Remove the saucepan from the heat, cover it and let it stand for 1 hour. Drain off the water and place the beans in the **CROCK-POT**® slow cooker.

Even presoaked beans take a long time to cook. Avoid adding acidic ingredients or sweeteners to the beans until they're soft, because this lengthens their cooking time. Acidic ingredients include tomatoes, vinegar, and citrus juices. Sweeteners include sugar, honey, and molasses. Add these items toward the end of the cooking time.

Top
Best-Loved
Dishes

Cook all your favorite meals in your slow cooker

Fall-Off-the-Bone Ribs

Makes 6 to 8 servings

½ cup paprika
⅜ cup sugar
¼ cup onion powder
1½ teaspoons salt
1½ teaspoons black pepper
2½ pounds pork baby back ribs, skinned
1 can (20 ounces) beer or beef stock
1 quart barbecue sauce
½ cup honey
White sesame seeds and sliced chives (optional)

1. Lightly oil grill grate and preheat on HIGH.

2. While grill heats, combine paprika, sugar, onion powder, salt and pepper in large mixing bowl. Generously season ribs with dry rub mixture. Place ribs on grill. Cook for 3 minutes on each side or until ribs have grill marks.

3. Portion ribs into sections of 3 to 4 bones. Place in 5-quart **CROCK-POT**® slow cooker. Pour beer over ribs. Cover; cook on HIGH 2 hours. Blend barbecue sauce and honey and add. Cover; cook for 1½ hours. Garnish with white sesame seeds and chives, if desired. Serve with extra sauce on the side.

Classic Spaghetti

Makes 6 to 8 servings

- 2 tablespoons olive oil
- 2 onions, chopped
- 2 green bell peppers, sliced
- 2 stalks celery, sliced
- 4 teaspoons minced garlic
- 3 pounds lean ground beef
- 2 carrots, diced
- 1 cup mushrooms, sliced
- 1 can (28 ounces) tomato sauce
- 3 cups water
- 1 can (28 ounces) stewed tomatoes, undrained
- 2 tablespoons minced parsley
- 1 tablespoon dried oregano
- 1 tablespoon sugar
- 2 teaspoons salt
- 2 teaspoons black pepper
- 1 pound dry spaghetti

1. Heat oil in large skillet over medium-high heat until hot. Add onions, bell peppers, celery and garlic; cook and stir until tender. Transfer to **CROCK-POT**® slow cooker.

2. In same skillet, brown ground beef. Drain and discard fat.

3. Add beef, carrots, mushrooms, tomato sauce, water, tomatoes with juice, parsley, oregano, sugar, salt and black pepper to **CROCK-POT**® slow cooker. Cover; cook on LOW 6 to 8 hours or on HIGH 3 to 5 hours, or until done.

4. Cook spaghetti according to package directions; drain. Serve sauce over cooked spaghetti.

Mama's Best Baked Beans

Makes 4 to 6 servings

- 1 bag (1 pound) dried Great Northern beans
- 1 package (1 pound) bacon
- 5 hot dogs, cut into ½-inch pieces
- 1 cup chopped onion
- 1 bottle (24 ounces) ketchup
- 2 cups packed dark brown sugar

1. Soak and cook beans according to package directions. Drain and refrigerate until ready to use.

2. Cook bacon in large skillet over medium-high heat until crisp. Transfer to paper towels to drain. Cool, then crumble bacon; set aside. Discard all but 3 tablespoons bacon fat from skillet. Add hot dogs and onion. Cook and stir over medium heat until onion is tender.

3. Combine cooked beans, bacon, hot dog mixture, ketchup and brown sugar in **CROCK-POT®** slow cooker. Cover; cook on LOW 2 to 4 hours.

Macaroni and Cheese

Makes 6 to 8 servings

- 6 cups cooked macaroni
- 2 tablespoons butter, melted
- 4 cups evaporated milk
- 6 cups Cheddar cheese, shredded
- 2 teaspoons salt
- ½ teaspoon black pepper

In large mixing bowl, toss macaroni with butter. Stir in evaporated milk, cheese, salt and pepper; place in **CROCK-POT®** slow cooker. Cover; cook on HIGH 2 to 3 hours.

Mama's Best Baked Beans

The Best Beef Stew

Makes 8 servings

½ cup plus 2 tablespoons all-purpose flour, divided

2 teaspoons salt

1 teaspoon black pepper

3 pounds beef for stew, cut into 1-inch pieces

1 can (16 ounces) diced tomatoes in juice, undrained

3 red potatoes, peeled and diced

½ pound smoked sausage, sliced

1 cup chopped leek

1 cup chopped onion

4 ribs celery, sliced

½ cup chicken broth

3 cloves garlic, minced

1 teaspoon dried thyme

3 tablespoons water

1. Combine ½ cup flour, salt and pepper in resealable plastic food storage bag. Add beef; shake bag to coat beef. Place beef in **CROCK-POT**® slow cooker.

2. Add remaining ingredients, except remaining 2 tablespoons flour and water; stir well. Cover; cook on LOW 8 to 12 hours or on HIGH 4 to 6 hours.

3. One hour before serving, turn **CROCK-POT**® slow cooker to HIGH. Combine remaining 2 tablespoons flour and water in small bowl; stir until mixture becomes paste. Stir mixture into stew; mix well. Cover; cook until thickened.

Tip: *For faster cooking time and more tender beef, brown flour-coated beef in 2 tablespoons olive oil in a large skillet over medium heat. Drain, then add browned beef to the remaining ingredients in the* **CROCK-POT**® *slow cooker. Cook on HIGH 3 to 5 hours or until tender.*

Slow-Cooked Pot Roast

Makes 6 to 8 servings

1   tablespoon vegetable oil
1   beef brisket (3 to 4 pounds)
1   tablespoon garlic powder, divided
1   tablespoon salt, divided
1   tablespoon black pepper, divided
1   teaspoon paprika, divided
5   to 6 new potatoes, cut into quarters
4   to 5 medium onions, sliced
1   pound baby carrots
1   can (14½ ounces) beef broth

1. Heat oil on HIGH in **CROCK-POT**® slow cooker. Brown brisket on all sides. Transfer brisket to plate. Season with 1½ teaspoons garlic powder, 1½ teaspoons salt, 1½ teaspoons pepper and ½ teaspoon paprika; set aside.

2. Season potatoes with remaining 1½ teaspoons garlic powder, 1½ teaspoons salt, 1½ teaspoons pepper and ½ teaspoon paprika. Add potatoes and onions to **CROCK-POT**® slow cooker. Cook on HIGH, stirring occasionally, until browned.

3. Return brisket to **CROCK-POT**® slow cooker. Add carrots and broth. Cover; cook on HIGH 4 to 5 hours or on LOW 8 to 10 hours, or until beef is tender.

Tip: Because **CROCK-POT**® slow cookers cook at a low heat for a long time, they're perfect for dishes calling for less tender cuts of meat.

Mom's Tuna Casserole

Makes 8 servings

- **2 cans (12 ounces each) tuna, drained and flaked**
- **3 cups diced celery**
- **3 cups crushed potato chips, divided**
- **6 hard-cooked eggs, chopped**
- **1 can (10¾ ounces) condensed cream of mushroom soup, undiluted**
- **1 can (10¾ ounces) condensed cream of celery soup, undiluted**
- **1 cup mayonnaise**
- **1 teaspoon dried tarragon**
- **1 teaspoon black pepper**

1. Combine tuna, celery, 2½ cups potato chips, eggs, soups, mayonnaise, tarragon and pepper in **CROCK-POT®** slow cooker; stir well. Cover; cook on LOW 5 to 8 hours.

2. Sprinkle with remaining ½ cup potato chips before serving.

*Tip: Don't use your **CROCK-POT®** slow cooker to reheat leftover foods. Transfer cooled leftover food to a resealable plastic food storage bag or plastic storage container with a tight-fitting lid and refrigerate. Use a microwave oven, the stove top or the oven for reheating.*

BBQ Beef Sandwiches

Makes 10 to 12 servings

- 1 **boneless beef chuck roast (about 3 pounds)**
- ¼ **cup ketchup**
- 2 **tablespoons brown sugar**
- 2 **tablespoons red wine vinegar**
- 1 **tablespoon Dijon mustard**
- 1 **tablespoon Worcestershire sauce**
- 1 **clove garlic, crushed**
- ¼ **teaspoon salt**
- ¼ **teaspoon liquid smoke**
- ⅛ **teaspoon black pepper**
- 10 **to 12 French rolls or sandwich buns, sliced in half**

1. Place beef in **CROCK-POT**® slow cooker. Combine remaining ingredients, except rolls, in medium bowl; pour over meat. Cover; cook on LOW 8 to 9 hours.

2. Remove beef from **CROCK-POT**® slow cooker; shred with 2 forks.

3. Combine beef with 1 cup sauce from **CROCK-POT**® slow cooker. Evenly distribute meat and sauce mixture among warmed rolls.

Tip: *To reduce the amount of fat in* **CROCK-POT**® *slow cooker meals, trim and discard excess fat from meats, or choose lean cuts.*

Vegetable-Stuffed Pork Chops

Makes 4 servings

4   **double pork rib chops, well trimmed**
    Salt and black pepper, to taste
1   **can (15¼ ounces) kernel corn, drained**
1   **green bell pepper, chopped**
1   **cup Italian-style seasoned dry bread crumbs**
1   **small onion, chopped**
½   **cup uncooked converted long-grain rice**
1   **can (8 ounces) tomato sauce**

1. Cut pocket into each pork chop, cutting from edge nearest bone. Lightly season pockets with salt and pepper to taste. Combine corn, bell pepper, bread crumbs, onion and rice in large bowl. Stuff pork chops with rice mixture. Secure open side with toothpicks.

2. Place any remaining rice mixture in **CROCK-POT**® slow cooker. Add stuffed pork chops to **CROCK-POT**® slow cooker. Moisten top of each pork chop with tomato sauce. Pour in any remaining tomato sauce. Cover; cook on LOW 8 to 10 hours.

3. Transfer pork chops to serving platter. Remove and discard toothpicks. Serve with extra rice mixture.

Tip: *Your butcher can cut a pocket in the pork chops to save you time and to ensure even cooking.*

Like Grandma's Chicken 'n Dumplings

Makes 4 to 6 servings

- 2 cups cooked chicken
- 1 can (10¾ ounces) condensed cream of mushroom soup, undiluted
- 1 can (10¾ ounces) condensed cream of chicken soup, undiluted
- 2 soup cans water
- 4 teaspoons all-purpose flour
- 2 teaspoons chicken bouillon granules
- ½ teaspoon black pepper
- 1 can refrigerated buttermilk biscuits (8 biscuits)

1. Mix all ingredients, except biscuits, in **CROCK-POT**® slow cooker.

2. Cut biscuits into quarters and gently stir into mixture. Cover; cook on LOW 4 to 6 hours.

*Tip: Don't add water to the **CROCK-POT**® slow cooker, unless the recipe specifically says to do so. Foods don't lose as much moisture during slow cooking as they can during conventional cooking, so follow the recipe guidelines for best results.*

Round Steak

Makes 4 servings

1   boneless beef round steak
     (1½ pounds), trimmed
     and cut into 4 pieces
¼   cup all-purpose flour
1   teaspoon black pepper
½   teaspoon salt
1   tablespoon vegetable oil
1   can (10¾ ounces) condensed
     cream of mushroom soup,
     undiluted
¾   cup water
1   medium onion, quartered
1   can (4 ounces) sliced
     mushrooms, drained
¼   cup milk
1   package (1 ounce) dry onion soup mix
1   bay leaf
     Seasonings, to taste: Salt, black pepper, ground sage, dried thyme

1. Place steak in large resealable plastic food storage bag. Close bag and pound with meat mallet to tenderize steak. Combine flour, 1 teaspoon pepper and ½ teaspoon salt in small bowl; add to bag with steaks. Shake to coat meat evenly.

2. Heat oil in large skillet over medium-high heat until hot. Remove steak from bag; shake off excess flour. Add steak to skillet; brown both sides. Transfer steak and pan juices to **CROCK-POT**® slow cooker.

3. Add canned soup, water, onion, mushrooms, milk, dry soup mix, bay leaf and seasonings, to taste, to **CROCK-POT**® slow cooker; mix well. Cover; cook on LOW 5 to 6 hours or until steak is tender. Remove and discard bay leaf before serving.

*Tip: Browning meat before cooking it in the **CROCK-POT**® slow cooker isn't necessary but helps to enhance the flavor and appearance of the finished dish.*

Italian Sausage and Peppers

Makes 4 servings

- 3 cups bell pepper chunks (1 inch), preferably a mix of red, yellow and green
- 1 small onion, cut into thin wedges
- 3 cloves garlic, minced
- 4 links hot or mild Italian sausage (about 1 pound)
- 1 cup marinara or pasta sauce
- ¼ cup red wine or port
- 1 tablespoon cornstarch
- 1 tablespoon water
   Hot cooked spaghetti
- ¼ cup grated Parmesan or Romano cheese

1. Coat **CROCK-POT**® slow cooker with nonstick cooking spray. Add bell peppers, onion and garlic. Arrange sausage over vegetables.

2. Combine pasta sauce and wine; pour over sausage. Cover; cook on LOW 8 to 9 hours or on HIGH 4 to 5 hours, or until sausage is cooked through and vegetables are very tender.

3. Transfer sausage to serving platter; cover with foil to keep warm. Skim off and discard fat from cooking liquid.

4. Turn heat to HIGH. Mix cornstarch with water until smooth; add to **CROCK-POT**® slow cooker. Cook 15 minutes or until sauce has thickened, stirring once. Serve sauce over spaghetti and sausage; top with cheese.

Tip: Look for mixed bell pepper chunks at supermarket salad bars.

Slow Cooker Pepper Steak

Makes 6 to 8 servings

2 tablespoons vegetable oil
3 pounds boneless beef top sirloin steak, cut into strips
1 tablespoon minced garlic (5 to 6 cloves)
1 medium onion, chopped
½ cup reduced-sodium soy sauce
2 teaspoons sugar
1 teaspoon salt
½ teaspoon ground ginger
½ teaspoon black pepper
3 green bell peppers, cut into strips
¼ cup cold water
1 tablespoon cornstarch
   Hot cooked white rice

1. Heat oil in large skillet over medium-low heat. Brown steak strips in 2 batches. Add garlic; cook and stir 2 minutes. Transfer steak strips, garlic and pan juices to **CROCK-POT**® slow cooker.

2. Add onion, soy sauce, sugar, salt, ginger and black pepper to **CROCK-POT**® slow cooker; mix well. Cover; cook on LOW 6 to 8 hours or until meat is tender (up to 10 hours). Add bell pepper strips during final hour of cooking.

3. Blend water and cornstarch until smooth; stir into **CROCK-POT**® slow cooker. Cook, uncovered, on HIGH 15 minutes or until thickened. Serve with rice.

*Tip: Cooking times are guidelines. **CROCK-POT**® slow cookers, just like ovens, cook differently depending on a variety of factors. For example, cooking times will be longer at higher altitudes. You may need to slightly adjust cooking times for your **CROCK-POT**® slow cooker.*

Slow Cooker Stuffed Peppers

Makes 4 servings

- 1 **package (about 7 ounces) Spanish rice mix**
- 1 **pound lean ground beef**
- ½ **cup diced celery**
- 1 **small onion, chopped**
- 1 **egg, beaten**
- 4 **medium green bell peppers, halved lengthwise, cored and seeded**
- 1 **can (28 ounces) whole peeled tomatoes, undrained**
- 1 **can (10¾ ounces) condensed tomato soup, undiluted**
- 1 **cup water**

1. Set aside seasoning packet from rice. Combine rice mix, beef, celery, onion and egg in large bowl. Divide meat mixture evenly among bell pepper halves.

2. Pour tomatoes with juice into **CROCK-POT**® slow cooker. Arrange filled bell pepper halves on top of tomatoes.

3. Combine tomato soup, water and reserved rice-mix seasoning packet in medium bowl. Pour over bell peppers. Cover; cook on LOW 8 to 10 hours.

Tip: Keep the lid on! The CROCK-POT® slow cooker can take as long as 30 minutes to regain the heat lost when the cover is removed. Only remove the cover when you're instructed to do so by the recipe.

Old World Chicken and Vegetables

Makes 4 servings

1   tablespoon dried oregano
1   teaspoon salt, divided
1   teaspoon paprika
½   teaspoon garlic powder
¼   teaspoon black pepper
2   medium green bell peppers,
    cut into thin strips
1   small yellow onion, thinly sliced
1   cut-up whole chicken
    (about 3 pounds)
⅓   cup ketchup
    Hot cooked egg noodles

1. Combine oregano, ½ teaspoon salt, paprika, garlic powder and black pepper in small bowl; mix well.

2. Place bell peppers and onion in **CROCK-POT**® slow cooker. Add chicken thighs and legs, and sprinkle with half of oregano mixture. Add chicken breasts, and sprinkle on remaining oregano mixture. Cover; cook on LOW 8 hours or on HIGH 4 hours. Stir in ketchup and remaining ½ teaspoon salt.

3. Serve chicken and vegetables over noodles.

Vegetarian Lasagna

Makes 4 to 6 servings

- 1 small eggplant, sliced into ½-inch rounds
- ½ teaspoon salt
- 2 tablespoons olive oil, divided
- 1 tablespoon butter
- 8 ounces mushrooms, sliced
- 1 small onion, diced
- 1 can (26 ounces) pasta sauce
- 1 teaspoon dried basil
- 1 teaspoon dried oregano
- 2 cups part-skim ricotta cheese
- 1½ cups (6 ounces) shredded Monterey Jack cheese
- 1 cup grated Parmesan cheese, divided
- 1 package (8 ounces) whole-wheat lasagna noodles, cooked and drained
- 1 medium zucchini, thinly sliced

1. Sprinkle eggplant with salt; let stand 10 to 15 minutes. Rinse off excess salt and pat dry; brush with 1 tablespoon olive oil. Brown on both sides in medium skillet over medium heat. Transfer to plate.

2. Heat remaining 1 tablespoon olive oil and butter in same skillet over medium heat; cook and stir mushrooms and onion until softened. Stir in pasta sauce, basil and oregano; set aside.

3. Combine ricotta cheese, Monterey Jack cheese and ½ cup Parmesan cheese in medium bowl; set aside.

4. Spread ⅓ sauce mixture in bottom of **CROCK-POT**® slow cooker. Layer with ⅓ lasagna noodles, ½ eggplant, ½ cheese mixture. Repeat layers. For last layer, use remaining ⅓ of lasagna noodles, zucchini, remaining ⅓ of sauce mixture and top with remaining ½ cup Parmesan cheese.

5. Cover; cook on LOW 6 hours. Let stand 15 to 20 minutes before serving.

Entertaining
Appetizers

Tasty finger foods for any occasion

Warm Blue Crab Bruschetta

Makes 16 servings

- 4 cups peeled, seeded and diced Roma or plum tomatoes
- 1 cup diced white onion
- 2 teaspoons minced garlic
- 1/3 cup olive oil
- 2 tablespoons balsamic vinegar
- 1/2 teaspoon dried oregano
- 2 tablespoons sugar
- 1 pound lump blue crabmeat, picked over for shells
- 1 1/2 teaspoons kosher salt
- 1/2 teaspoon cracked black pepper
- 1/3 cup minced fresh basil
- 2 baguettes, sliced and toasted

1. Combine tomatoes, onion, garlic, oil, vinegar, oregano and sugar in **CROCK-POT**® slow cooker. Cover; cook on LOW 2 hours.

2. Add crabmeat, salt and pepper. Stir gently to mix, taking care not to break up crabmeat lumps. Cook on LOW 1 hour.

3. Fold in basil. Serve on toasted baguette slices.

Tip: Crab appetizer also can be served with Melba toast or whole-grain crackers.

Maple-Glazed Meatballs

Makes about 48 meatballs

1½ **cups ketchup**
1 **cup maple syrup** *or* **maple-flavored syrup**
⅓ **cup reduced-sodium soy sauce**
1 **tablespoon quick-cooking tapioca**
1½ **teaspoons ground allspice**
1 **teaspoon dry mustard**
2 **packages (about 16 ounces each) frozen fully cooked meatballs, partially thawed and separated**
1 **can (20 ounces) pineapple chunks in juice, drained**

1. Combine ketchup, maple syrup, soy sauce, tapioca, allspice and mustard in **CROCK-POT®** slow cooker.

2. Carefully stir meatballs and pineapple chunks into ketchup mixture.

3. Cover; cook on LOW 5 to 6 hours. Stir before serving. Serve warm; insert cocktail picks, if desired.

Tip: *For a quick main dish, serve meatballs over hot cooked rice.*

Creamy Cheesy Spinach Dip

Makes about 4 cups

2   packages (10 ounces each) frozen chopped spinach, thawed
2   cups chopped onions
1   teaspoon salt
½   teaspoon garlic powder
¼   teaspoon black pepper
12 ounces pasteurized processed cheese spread with jalapeño peppers, cubed
    Cherry tomatoes with pulp removed (optional)
    Sliced cucumbers (optional)
    Assorted crackers (optional)

1. Drain spinach and squeeze dry, reserving ¾ cup liquid. Place spinach, reserved liquid, onions, salt, garlic powder and pepper into 1½-quart or other small-sized **CROCK-POT**® slow cooker; stir to blend. Cover; cook on HIGH 1½ hours.

2. Stir in cheese and cook 30 minutes longer or until melted. Fill cherry tomato shells, spread on cucumber slices or serve with crackers, if desired.

Tip: To thaw spinach quickly, remove paper wrapper from spinach containers. Microwave on HIGH 3 to 4 minutes or until just thawed.

Easiest Three-Cheese Fondue

Makes 8 servings

2 cups (8 ounces) shredded mild or sharp Cheddar cheese
¾ cup reduced-fat (2%) milk
½ cup (2 ounces) crumbled blue cheese
1 package (3 ounces) cream cheese, cut into cubes
¼ cup finely chopped onion
1 tablespoon all-purpose flour
1 tablespoon butter or margarine
2 cloves garlic, minced
4 to 6 drops hot pepper sauce
⅛ teaspoon ground red pepper
Breadsticks and assorted fresh vegetables for dipping

1. Combine all ingredients, except breadsticks and vegetables, in **CROCK-POT®** slow cooker. Cover; cook on LOW 2 to 2½ hours, stirring once or twice, until cheese is melted and smooth.

2. Increase heat to HIGH. Cook 1 to 1½ hours or until heated through. Serve with breadsticks and fresh vegetables for dipping.

Tip: To reduce the total fat in this recipe, use reduced-fat Cheddar cheese and Neufchâtel cheese instead of full-fat cream cheese.

Asian-Spiced Chicken Wings

Makes 10 to 16 appetizers

- **3** pounds chicken wings
- **1** cup packed light brown sugar
- **1** cup soy sauce
- **½** cup ketchup
- **2** teaspoons fresh ginger, minced
- **2** cloves garlic, minced
- **¼** cup dry sherry
- **½** cup hoisin sauce
- **1** tablespoon fresh lime juice
- **3** tablespoons sesame seeds, toasted
- **¼** cup green onions, thinly sliced

1. Preheat broiler. Place chicken wings on broiler pan. Broil 4 to 5 inches from heat 10 minutes per side, or until wings are brown. Transfer to **CROCK-POT®** slow cooker.

2. Add sugar, soy sauce, ketchup, ginger, garlic and sherry; stir thoroughly to coat wings. Cover; cook on LOW 5 to 6 hours or on HIGH 2 to 3 hours or until chicken wings are no longer pink, stirring once halfway through cooking time to baste wings with sauce.

3. Remove wings from **CROCK-POT®** slow cooker. Reserve ¼ cup of cooking liquid; combine with hoisin sauce and lime juice. Drizzle mixture over chicken wings. Sprinkle with sesame seeds and green onions before serving.

Tip: For 5-, 6-, or 7-quart **CROCK-POT®** slow cookers, increase amount of chicken wings to 5 pounds.

Honey-Sauced Chicken Wings

Makes 24 to 32 appetizers

3 pounds chicken wings
1 teaspoon salt
½ teaspoon black pepper
1 cup honey
½ cup soy sauce
¼ cup chopped onion
¼ cup ketchup
2 tablespoons vegetable oil
2 cloves garlic, minced
¼ teaspoon red pepper flakes
Toasted sesame seeds
(optional)

1. Preheat broiler. Cut off and discard chicken wing tips. Cut each wing at joint to make 2 sections. Sprinkle wing parts with salt and pepper. Place on broiler pan. Broil 4 to 5 inches from heat about 10 minutes per side, or until chicken wings are brown. Transfer to **CROCK-POT**® slow cooker.

2. For sauce, combine honey, soy sauce, onion, ketchup, oil, garlic and pepper flakes in bowl. Pour over chicken wings.

3. Cover; cook on LOW 4 to 5 hours or on HIGH 2 to 2½ hours. Garnish with sesame seeds, if desired.

Tip: Consider using your **CROCK-POT**® *slow cooker as an "extra" oven or burner when entertaining. For example, the* **CROCK-POT**® *slow cooker can cook other dishes while the holiday roast is in the oven.*

Slow Cooker Cheese Dip

Makes 16 to 18 servings

- 1 pound 95% lean ground beef
- 1 pound bulk Italian sausage
- 1 package (16 ounces) pasteurized processed cheese spread, cubed
- 1 can (11 ounces) sliced jalapeño peppers, drained
- 1 medium onion, diced
- 8 ounces Cheddar cheese, cubed
- 1 package (8 ounces) cream cheese, cubed
- 1 container (8 ounces) cottage cheese
- 1 container (8 ounces) sour cream
- 1 can (8 ounces) diced tomatoes, drained
- 3 cloves garlic, minced
  Salt and pepper, to taste

1. Brown ground beef and sausage in medium skillet over medium-high heat, stirring to break up meat. Drain and discard fat. Transfer to **CROCK-POT**® slow cooker.

2. Add processed cheese, jalapeño peppers, onion, Cheddar cheese, cream cheese, cottage cheese, sour cream, tomatoes and garlic to **CROCK-POT**® slow cooker. Season with salt and pepper.

3. Cover; cook on HIGH 1½ to 2 hours or until cheeses are melted. Serve with crackers or tortilla chips.

Tip: *To reduce the total fat in this recipe, use reduced-fat Cheddar cheese and Neufchâtel cheese instead of full-fat cream cheese.*

Angel Wings

Makes 10 appetizers

1	can (10¾ ounces) condensed tomato soup, undiluted
¾	cup water
¼	cup packed light brown sugar
2½	tablespoons balsamic vinegar
2	tablespoons chopped shallots
10	chicken wings

1. Combine soup, water, brown sugar, vinegar and shallots in **CROCK-POT**® slow cooker; mix well.

2. Add chicken wings; stir to coat with sauce. Cover; cook on LOW 5 to 6 hours or until cooked through and glazed with sauce.

Tip: *To reheat leftover foods, don't use the **CROCK-POT**® slow cooker. Transfer cooled leftovers to a resealable plastic food storage bag or plastic storage container with a tight-fitting lid and refrigerate. Use a microwave oven, the stove top or an oven for reheating.*

Easy Taco Dip

Makes about 3 cups

- ½ **pound 95% lean ground beef**
- 1 **cup frozen corn**
- ½ **cup chopped onion**
- ½ **cup salsa**
- ½ **cup mild taco sauce**
- 1 **can (4 ounces) diced mild green chilies**
- 1 **can (4 ounces) sliced ripe olives, drained**
- 1 **cup (4 ounces) shredded Mexican cheese blend**
  Tortilla chips
  Sour cream

1. Brown ground beef in large nonstick skillet over medium-high heat, stirring to break up meat. Drain and discard fat. Transfer to **CROCK-POT**® slow cooker.

2. Add corn, onion, salsa, taco sauce, chilies and olives; mix well. Cover; cook on LOW 2 to 3 hours.

3. Just before serving, stir in cheese. Serve with tortilla chips and sour cream.

*Tip: To keep this dip hot through an entire party, leave it in the **CROCK-POT**® slow cooker on the LOW or WARM setting.*

Cocktail Meatballs

Makes about 24 meatballs

1   pound 95% lean ground beef
1   pound bulk pork or Italian sausage
1   cup cracker crumbs
1   cup finely chopped onion
1   cup finely chopped green bell pepper
½   cup milk
1   egg, beaten
2   teaspoons salt
1   teaspoon dried Italian seasoning
¼   teaspoon black pepper
1   cup ketchup
¾   cup packed dark brown sugar
½   cup (1 stick) butter or margarine
½   cup vinegar
¼   cup lemon juice
¼   cup water
1   teaspoon prepared mustard
¼   teaspoon garlic salt

1. Preheat oven to 350°F. Combine beef, pork, cracker crumbs, onion, bell pepper, milk, egg, salt, Italian seasoning and pepper in bowl. Mix well; form into 1-inch meatballs. Place meatballs onto 2 nonstick baking sheets. Bake 25 minutes or until browned.

2. Meanwhile, place ketchup, sugar, butter, vinegar, lemon juice, water, mustard and garlic salt into **CROCK-POT**® slow cooker; mix well. Cover; cook on HIGH 15 to 20 minutes or until hot.

3. Transfer meatballs to **CROCK-POT**® slow cooker; carefully stir to coat with sauce. Reduce heat to LOW. Cover; cook 2 hours.

Bacon and Cheese Dip

Makes 16 servings (about 4 cups)

- **2** packages (8 ounces each) reduced-fat cream cheese, softened and cut into cubes
- **4** cups (16 ounces) shredded reduced-fat sharp Cheddar cheese
- **1** cup evaporated skim milk
- **2** tablespoons prepared mustard
- **1** tablespoon chopped onion
- **2** teaspoons Worcestershire sauce
- **½** teaspoon salt
- **¼** teaspoon hot pepper sauce
- **1** pound turkey bacon, crisp-cooked and crumbled
    Assorted cut-up vegetables (optional)
    Crusty French or Italian bread, sliced (optional)
    Assorted crackers (optional)

1. Place cream cheese, Cheddar cheese, evaporated milk, mustard, onion, Worcestershire sauce, salt and hot sauce in **CROCK-POT**® slow cooker. Cover; cook on LOW, stirring occasionally, 1 hour or until cheese melts.

2. Stir in bacon; adjust seasonings as desired. Serve with vegetable dippers, crusty bread or assorted crackers.

Tip: *When adapting your own recipes for the **CROCK-POT**® slow cooker, use canned evaporated milk, nonfat dry milk or undiluted condensed soups instead of milk to make smooth dips and sauces.*

Red Pepper Relish

Makes 8 servings

4 large red bell peppers, cut into thin strips
2 small Vidalia or other sweet onions, thinly sliced
6 tablespoons cider vinegar
¼ cup packed light brown sugar
2 tablespoons vegetable oil
2 tablespoons honey
½ teaspoon salt
½ teaspoon dried thyme
½ teaspoon red pepper flakes
½ teaspoon black pepper
2 baguettes, sliced and toasted

Combine all ingredients, except baguettes, in **CROCK-POT®** slow cooker; mix well. Cover; cook on LOW 4 hours. Serve on toasted baguette slices.

Teriyaki Chicken Wings

Makes 6 to 8 servings

3 to 4 pounds chicken wings
¼ cup soy sauce
¼ cup sherry
¼ cup honey
1 tablespoon hoisin sauce
1 tablespoon orange juice
2 cloves garlic, minced

Place wings in **CROCK-POT®** slow cooker. Blend remaining ingredients in medium bowl; pour over wings. Cover; cook on HIGH 1½ to 2 hours or on LOW 3 to 3½ hours.

Hearty Calico Bean Dip

Makes 12 servings

- ¾ **pound 95% lean ground beef**
- ½ **pound sliced bacon, crisp-cooked and crumbled**
- 1 **can (16 ounces) baked beans**
- 1 **can (15 ounces) Great Northern beans, rinsed and drained**
- 1 **can (15 ounces) kidney beans, rinsed and drained**
- 1 **small onion, chopped**
- ½ **cup packed dark brown sugar**
- ½ **cup ketchup**
- 1 **tablespoon cider vinegar**
- 1 **teaspoon prepared mustard**
  Tortilla chips

1. Brown ground beef in large nonstick skillet over medium-high heat, stirring to break up meat. Drain and discard fat. Transfer to **CROCK-POT**® slow cooker.

2. Add bacon, beans, onion, sugar, ketchup, vinegar and mustard; mix well.

3. Cover; cook on LOW 4 hours or on HIGH 2 hours. Serve with tortilla chips.

Tip: *For a party, use a small-sized **CROCK-POT**® slow cooker (1 quart or 1½ quarts) on the LOW or WARM setting to keep hot dips warm.*

Pizza Fondue

Makes 20 to 25 appetizer servings

½ **pound bulk Italian sausage**
1 **cup chopped onion**
2 **jars (26 ounces each) meatless pasta sauce**
4 **ounces thinly sliced ham, finely chopped**
1 **package (3 ounces) sliced pepperoni, finely chopped**
¼ **teaspoon red pepper flakes**
1 **pound mozzarella cheese, cut into ¾-inch cubes**
1 **loaf Italian or French bread, cut into 1-inch cubes**

1. Cook and stir sausage and onion in large skillet over medium-high heat until sausage is browned. Drain and discard fat.

2. Transfer sausage mixture to **CROCK-POT**® slow cooker. Stir in pasta sauce, ham, pepperoni and pepper flakes. Cover; cook on LOW 3 to 4 hours. Serve warm fondue with mozzarella cheese and bread cubes.

Creamy Artichoke-Parmesan Dip

Makes 16 servings (about 4 cups)

- **2 cans (14 ounces each) artichoke hearts, drained and chopped**
- **2 cups (8 ounces) shredded mozzarella cheese**
- **1½ cups grated Parmesan cheese**
- **1½ cups mayonnaise**
- **½ cup finely chopped onion**
- **½ teaspoon dried oregano**
- **¼ teaspoon garlic powder**
- **4 pita breads, cut into wedges**
  Assorted cut-up vegetables

Place artichokes, mozzarella cheese, Parmesan cheese, mayonnaise, onion, oregano and garlic powder in 1½-quart or other small-sized **CROCK-POT®** slow cooker; mix well. Cover; cook on LOW 2 hours. Arrange pita bread wedges and vegetables on platter; serve with warm dip.

Tip: When adapting conventionally prepared recipes for your **CROCK-POT®** slow cooker, revise the amount of herbs and spices you use. For example, whole herbs and spices increase in flavor while ground spices tend to lose flavor during slow cooking. You can adjust the seasonings or add fresh herbs and spices just before serving the dish.

Crowd
Pleasers

Let your slow cooker do the work

Barbecued Pulled Pork Sandwiches

Makes 8 servings

1   pork shoulder roast (about 2½ pounds)
1   bottle (14 ounces) barbecue sauce
1   tablespoon fresh lemon juice
1   teaspoon brown sugar
1   medium onion, chopped
8   hamburger buns or hard rolls

1. Place roast in **CROCK-POT**® slow cooker. Cover; cook on LOW 10 to 12 hours or on HIGH 5 to 6 hours.

2. Remove roast from **CROCK-POT**® slow cooker; discard cooking liquid. Shred pork with 2 forks. Return pork to **CROCK-POT**® slow cooker. Add barbecue sauce, lemon juice, brown sugar and onion. Cover; cook on HIGH 1 hour or on LOW 2 hours. Serve shredded pork on hamburger buns or hard rolls.

*Tip: For 5-, 6-, or 7-quart **CROCK-POT**® slow cookers, double all ingredients, except barbecue sauce. Increase barbecue sauce to 21 ounces.*

Bean and Corn Chili

Makes 6 servings

2   tablespoons red wine
½   teaspoon olive oil
2   medium onions, finely chopped
5   cloves garlic, minced
1   green bell pepper, finely chopped
1   red bell pepper, finely chopped
1   rib celery, finely sliced
6   Roma or plum tomatoes, chopped
2   cans (15 ounces) kidney beans,
     rinsed and drained
1½ cups fat-free chicken or vegetable
     broth
1   can (6 ounces) tomato paste
1   cup frozen corn kernels
1   teaspoon salt
1   teaspoon chili powder
½   teaspoon black pepper
¼   teaspoon cumin
¼   teaspoon ground red pepper
¼   teaspoon dried oregano
¼   teaspoon ground coriander

1. Heat red wine and olive oil in medium skillet over medium heat until hot. Add onions and garlic; cook and stir until onions are tender. Transfer to **CROCK-POT**® slow cooker.

2. Add bell peppers, celery, tomatoes, beans, broth, tomato paste, corn, salt, chili powder, black pepper, cumin, red pepper, oregano and coriander. Mix well. Cover; cook on LOW 6 to 8 hours or on HIGH 3 to 4 hours.

Tip: *For 5-, 6-, or 7-quart* **CROCK-POT**® *slow cookers, double all ingredients.*

Hot Beef Sandwiches Au Jus

Makes 8 to 10 servings

- 4 pounds beef rump roast
- 2 envelopes (1 ounce each) dried onion soup mix
- 2 teaspoons sugar
- 1 teaspoon dried oregano
- 1 tablespoon minced garlic
- 2 cans (10½ ounces each) beef broth
- 1 bottle (12 ounces) beer
  Crusty French rolls, sliced in half

1. Trim excess fat from beef and discard. Place beef in **CROCK-POT**® slow cooker.

2. Combine soup mix, sugar, oregano, garlic, broth and beer in large mixing bowl. Pour mixture over beef. Cover; cook on HIGH 6 to 8 hours or until beef is fork-tender.

3. Remove beef from **CROCK-POT**® slow cooker. Shred beef with 2 forks. Return beef to cooking liquid; mix well. Serve on crusty rolls with extra cooking liquid ("jus") on side for dipping.

*Tip: One way to remove fat from any cooking liquids in **CROCK-POT**® slow cooker dishes is to refrigerate the liquid overnight. The fat will float to the top and solidify for easy removal.*

Spicy Asian Pork Filling

Makes 5½ cups

1   boneless pork sirloin roast (about 3 pounds)
½   cup tamari or other soy sauce
1   tablespoon chili garlic sauce *or* chili paste
2   teaspoons minced fresh ginger
2   tablespoons water
1   tablespoon cornstarch
2   teaspoons dark sesame oil

1. Cut roast into 2- to 3-inch chunks. Combine pork, tamari sauce, chili garlic sauce and ginger in **CROCK-POT®** slow cooker; mix well. Cover; cook on LOW 8 to 10 hours or until pork is fork-tender.

2. Remove roast from cooking liquid; cool slightly. Trim and discard excess fat. Shred pork with 2 forks. Let cooking liquid stand 5 minutes to allow fat to rise. Skim off and discard fat from cooking liquid.

3. Blend water, cornstarch and sesame oil until smooth; stir into **CROCK-POT®** slow cooker. Cook, uncovered, on HIGH until thickened. Add shredded meat to **CROCK-POT®** slow cooker; mix well. Cover; cook 15 to 30 minutes or until hot.

Serving Suggestions

SPICY ASIAN PORK BUNDLES: *Place ¼ cup pork filling into large lettuce leaves. Add shredded carrots, if desired. Wrap to enclose. Makes about 20 bundles.*

MU SHU PORK: *Lightly spread prepared plum sauce over small warm flour tortillas. Spoon ¼ cup pork filling and ¼ cup stir-fried vegetables into flour tortillas. Wrap to enclose. Serve immediately. Makes about 20 wraps.*

Sweet 'n Spicy Ribs

Makes 10 servings

- 5 **cups barbecue sauce**
- ¾ **cup packed dark brown sugar**
- ¼ **cup honey**
- 2 **tablespoons Cajun seasoning**
- 1 **tablespoon garlic powder**
- 1 **tablespoon onion powder**
- 6 **pounds pork or beef back ribs, cut into 3-rib portions**

1. Combine barbecue sauce, sugar, honey, Cajun seasoning, garlic powder and onion powder in medium bowl. Remove 1 cup mixture; refrigerate and reserve for dipping sauce.

2. Place ribs in large **CROCK-POT**® slow cooker. Pour barbecue sauce mixture over ribs. Cover; cook on LOW 8 hours or until meat is very tender.

3. Transfer ribs to serving platter; cover with foil to keep warm. Skim fat from sauce and discard. Serve ribs with additional reserved sauce.

Tip: *To remove a small amount of fat from dishes cooked in the **CROCK-POT**® slow cooker, lightly pull a sheet of clean paper towel over the surface, letting the grease be absorbed by the paper towel. Repeat this process as necessary.*

Company Slow Cooker Pork Chops

Makes 4 to 6 servings

- **2 tablespoons oil**
- **4 to 6 pork loin chops, cut ¾ inch thick**
  Black pepper, to taste
- **2 cans (10¾ ounces each) condensed fat-free cream of mushroom soup, undiluted**
- **½ cup skim milk**
- **1 package (3 ounces) low-fat cream cheese, softened**
- **¼ cup fat-free sour cream**
- **1 jar (2½ ounces) sliced dried beef**

1. Heat oil in large skillet over medium-high heat until hot. Brown pork chops on both sides. Season with pepper.

2. Coat **CROCK-POT®** slow cooker with nonstick cooking spray. Blend soup, milk, cream cheese and sour cream until smooth.

3. Place half of pork chops into **CROCK-POT®** slow cooker. Top with 4 slices dried beef. Pour half of sauce mixture over pork. Repeat with remaining chops, dried beef and sauce. Cover; cook on LOW 8 to 9 hours. Adjust seasoning before serving, if necessary.

Tip: Browning the pork before cooking it in the **CROCK-POT®** slow cooker isn't necessary but helps to enhance the flavor and appearance of the finished dish.

Creamy Slow Cooker Seafood Chowder

Makes 8 to 10 servings

1 quart (4 cups) half-and-half
2 cans (14½ ounces each) whole white potatoes, drained and cubed
2 cans (10¾ ounces) condensed cream of mushroom soup, undiluted
1 bag (16 ounces) frozen hash brown potatoes
1 medium onion, minced
½ cup (1 stick) butter, diced
1 teaspoon salt
1 teaspoon black pepper
5 cans (about 8 ounces each) whole oysters, drained and rinsed
2 cans (about 6 ounces each) minced clams
2 cans (about 4 ounces each) cocktail shrimp, drained and rinsed

1. Combine half-and-half, canned potatoes, soup, frozen potatoes, onion, butter, salt and pepper in 5-quart **CROCK-POT**® slow cooker. Mix well. Cover; cook on LOW 3½ to 4½ hours.

2. Add oysters, clams and shrimp; stir gently. Cover; cook on LOW 30 to 45 minutes, or until done.

*Tip: Seafood is delicate and should be added to the **CROCK-POT**® slow cooker during the last 15 to 30 minutes of the cooking time if you're using the HIGH heat setting, and during the last 30 to 45 minutes if you're using the LOW setting. Seafood overcooks easily, becoming tough and rubbery, so watch your cooking times, and cook only long enough for seafood to be done.*

Best Asian-Style Ribs

Makes 6 to 8 servings

2   full racks baby back pork ribs, split into 3 sections each
6   ounces hoisin sauce
2   tablespoons minced fresh ginger
½   cup maraschino cherries
½   cup rice wine vinegar
1   cup water
4   scallions or green onions, chopped

1. Combine ribs, hoisin sauce, ginger, cherries, vinegar and water in **CROCK-POT®** slow cooker. Cover; cook on LOW 6 to 7 hours or on HIGH 3 to 3½ hours, or until pork is done.

2. Remove ribs. Thicken sauce; heating uncovered or cook in saucepan until consistency of barbecue sauce. Sprinkle with scallions. Serve ribs with extra sauce.

Suzie's Sloppy Joes

Makes 8 servings

3	pounds 95% lean ground beef
1	cup chopped onion
3	cloves garlic, minced
1¼	cups ketchup
1	cup chopped red bell pepper
¼	cup plus 1 tablespoon Worcestershire sauce
¼	cup packed dark brown sugar
3	tablespoons prepared mustard
3	tablespoons vinegar
2	teaspoons chili powder
	Toasted hamburger buns

1. Cook and stir ground beef, onion and garlic in large nonstick skillet over medium-high heat until beef is browned and onion is tender. Drain and discard fat.

2. Combine ketchup, bell pepper, Worcestershire sauce, sugar, mustard, vinegar and chili powder in **CROCK-POT**® slow cooker. Stir in beef mixture. Cover; cook on LOW 6 to 8 hours. To serve, spoon mixture onto hamburger buns.

Tip: Don't worry about making big batches of food in your **CROCK-POT**® slow cooker. Instead, plan ahead to freeze the leftovers as individual portions. Just reheat a single serving in the microwave for fast meals or impulse snacks.

Bean Dip for a Crowd

Makes 24 servings (about 6 cups)

1½ cups dried black beans
1½ cups dried pinto beans
 5 cups water
 1 package (about 1¼ ounces) hot taco seasoning mix
 2 tablespoons dried minced onion
 3 chicken bouillon cubes
 1 tablespoon dried parsley flakes
 2 bay leaves
 1 jar (16 ounces) thick and chunky salsa (medium or hot)
 2 tablespoons lime juice

1. Place beans in large bowl; cover with water. Soak 6 to 8 hours or overnight. (To quick-soak beans, place beans in large saucepan; cover with water. Bring to a boil over high heat. Boil 2 minutes. Remove from heat; let soak, covered, 1 hour.) Drain beans; discard water.

2. Combine soaked beans, 5 cups water, taco seasoning, onion, bouillon cubes, parsley and bay leaves in **CROCK-POT**® slow cooker. Cover; cook on LOW 9 to 10 hours or until beans are tender. Add additional water, ½ cup at a time, if needed.

3. Remove and discard bay leaves. Ladle half of hot bean mixture into food processor. Add salsa and lime juice. Cover and process until smooth. Return puréed dip to **CROCK-POT**® slow cooker; stir to combine.

*Tip: You may substitute canned beans for the dried beans in this recipe. Canned beans are ideal for **CROCK-POT**® slow cookers because they're already soft. Because salt, sugar, and acidic ingredients can toughen dried beans as they cook, dried beans must be cooked and tender before you can add salt, sugar, or acidic ingredients.*

Spicy Italian Beef

Makes 8 to 10 servings

- 1   boneless beef chuck roast
       (3 to 4 pounds)
- 1   jar (12 ounces) pepperoncini
- 1   can (14½ ounces) beef broth
- 1   bottle (12 ounces) beer
- 1   onion, minced
- 2   tablespoons dried Italian seasoning
- 1   loaf French bread, cut into thick
       slices
- 10 slices provolone cheese (optional)

1. Trim fat from beef and discard. Cut beef, if necessary, to fit in **CROCK-POT**® slow cooker, leaving beef in as many large pieces as possible.

2. Drain pepperoncini; pull off stem ends and discard. Add pepperoncini, broth, beer, onion and herb blend to **CROCK-POT**® slow cooker; do not stir. Cover; cook on LOW 8 to 10 hours.

3. Remove beef from **CROCK-POT**® slow cooker; shred with 2 forks. Return shredded beef to cooking liquid; mix well. Serve on French bread, topped with cheese, if desired. Add additional sauce and pepperoncini, if desired.

Tip: Pepperoncini are thin 2- to 3-inch-long pickled mild peppers, available in the supermarket's Italian foods or pickled foods section.

Best Beef Brisket Sandwich Ever

Makes 10 to 12 servings

1 beef brisket (about 3 pounds)
2 cups apple cider, divided
1 head garlic, cloves separated, crushed and peeled
2 tablespoons whole peppercorns
⅓ cup chopped fresh thyme *or* 2 tablespoons dried thyme
1 tablespoon mustard seeds
1 tablespoon Cajun seasoning
1 teaspoon ground allspice
1 teaspoon ground cumin
1 teaspoon celery seeds
2 to 4 whole cloves
1 bottle (12 ounces) dark beer
10 to 12 sourdough sandwich rolls, sliced in half

1. Place brisket, ½ cup cider, garlic, peppercorns, thyme, mustard seeds, Cajun seasoning, allspice, cumin, celery seeds and cloves in large resealable food storage bag. Seal bag; marinate in refrigerator overnight.

2. Place brisket and marinade in **CROCK-POT**® slow cooker. Add remaining 1½ cups apple cider and beer. Cover; cook on LOW 10 hours or until brisket is tender.

3. Strain sauce; drizzle over meat. Slice brisket and place on sandwich rolls.

*Tip: Unless you have a 5-, 6-, or 7-quart **CROCK-POT**® slow cooker, cut any roast larger than 2½ pounds in half so it cooks completely.*

Brats in Beer

Makes 30 to 36 appetizers

1½ pounds bratwurst (about 5 or
    6 links)

1 bottle (12 ounces) amber ale or
    beer

1 medium onion, thinly sliced

2 tablespoons packed light brown
    sugar

2 tablespoons red wine or cider
    vinegar

    Spicy brown mustard

    Cocktail rye bread

1. Combine bratwurst, ale, onion, sugar and vinegar in **CROCK-POT®** slow cooker. Cover; cook on LOW 4 to 5 hours.

2. Remove bratwurst from cooking liquid. Cut into ½-inch-thick slices.

3. To make mini open-faced sandwiches, spread mustard on cocktail rye bread. Top with bratwurst slices and onion, if desired. (Whole brats also can be served on toasted split French or Italian rolls.)

Tip: Choose a light-tasting beer when cooking brats. Hearty ales can leave the meat tasting slightly bitter.

Slow Cooker Steak Fajitas

Makes 4 servings

1 beef flank steak
(about 1 pound)

1 medium onion, cut into strips

½ cup medium salsa, plus
additional for garnish

2 tablespoons chopped fresh
cilantro

2 tablespoons fresh lime juice

2 cloves garlic, minced

1 tablespoon chili powder

1 teaspoon ground cumin

½ teaspoon salt

1 small green bell pepper, cut
into strips

1 small red bell pepper, cut into
strips

Flour tortillas, warmed

1. Cut flank steak lengthwise in half, then crosswise into thin strips; place meat in **CROCK-POT**® slow cooker. Combine onion, ½ cup salsa, cilantro, lime juice, garlic, chili powder, cumin and salt in **CROCK-POT**® slow cooker. Cover; cook on LOW 5 to 6 hours.

2. Add bell peppers. Cover; cook on LOW 1 hour.

3. Serve with flour tortillas and additional salsa, if desired.

Tip: **CROCK-POT**® *slow cooker recipes calling for raw meats should cook a minimum of 3 hours on LOW for food safety reasons. When in doubt, use an instant-read thermometer to ensure the meat has reached the recommended internal temperature for safe consumption.*

Dilly Beef Sandwiches

Makes 6 to 8 servings

1   chuck beef roast (3 to 4 pounds)
1   jar (6 ounces) sliced dill pickles, undrained
1   can (14 ounces) crushed tomatoes with Italian seasoning
1   medium onion, diced
4   cloves garlic, minced
1   teaspoon mustard seeds
    Hamburger buns
    Optional toppings: lettuce, sliced tomatoes, sliced red onions

1. Trim excess fat from beef and discard. Cut beef into chunks. Place in **CROCK-POT**® slow cooker. Pour pickles with juice over beef. Add tomatoes, onion, garlic and mustard seeds. Cover; cook on LOW 8 to 10 hours.

2. Remove beef from **CROCK-POT**® slow cooker. Shred beef with 2 forks. Return beef to tomato mixture; mix well. Serve on toasted hamburger buns; top as desired.

Honey-Mustard Chicken Wings

Makes 4 to 5 servings

- **3 pounds chicken wings**
- **1 teaspoon salt**
- **1 teaspoon black pepper**
- **½ cup honey**
- **½ cup barbecue sauce**
- **2 tablespoons spicy brown mustard**
- **1 clove garlic, minced**
- **3 to 4 thin lemon slices**

1. Preheat broiler. Cut off wing tips; discard. Cut each wing at joint to make 2 pieces. Season with salt and pepper. Place on broiler pan. Broil 4 to 5 inches from heat about 5 minutes per side. Transfer to **CROCK-POT**® slow cooker.

2. Combine honey, barbecue sauce, mustard and garlic in small bowl; mix well. Pour sauce over chicken wings. Top with lemon slices. Cover; cook on LOW 4 to 5 hours. Before serving, remove and discard lemon slices. Serve wings with sauce.

Beef Chuck Chili

Makes 8 to 10 servings

 5 pounds beef chuck roast
½ cup plus 2 tablespoons olive oil, divided
 3 cups minced onions
 4 poblano peppers,* seeded and diced
 2 serrano peppers,* seeded and diced
 2 green bell peppers, seeded and diced
 3 jalapeño peppers,** seeded and diced
 2 tablespoons minced garlic
 1 can (28 ounces) crushed tomatoes
¼ cup hot pepper sauce
 1 tablespoon ground cumin
   Black pepper, to taste
 4 ounces Mexican lager beer (optional)
   Cornbread or hot cooked rice

*Handle fresh chili peppers as directed for jalapeño peppers. If fresh chili peppers are unavailable, use 2 cans (14 ounces each) diced green chilies and add dried ground chili powder for more heat.

**Jalapeño peppers can sting and irritate the skin. Wear rubber gloves when handling peppers and do not touch your eyes. Wash hands after handling peppers.

1. Trim excess fat from roast and discard. Heat ½ cup olive oil in large skillet over medium-high heat until hot. Add chuck roast; sear on both sides. Transfer beef to **CROCK-POT**® slow cooker.

2. Heat remaining 2 tablespoons oil in same skillet over low heat. Add onions, peppers and garlic; cook and stir about 7 minutes or until onions are tender. Transfer to **CROCK-POT**® slow cooker. Add crushed tomatoes. Cover; cook on LOW 4 to 5 hours or until beef is fork-tender.

3. Remove beef from **CROCK-POT**® slow cooker. Shred beef with 2 forks. Add hot sauce, cumin, black pepper and beer, if desired, to cooking liquid. Return beef to cooking liquid and mix well. Serve over cornbread or rice.

Quick Dinners

Prepare in the morning for delicious meals at night

Easy Cheesy BBQ Chicken

Makes 6 servings

6   boneless skinless chicken breasts (about 1½ pounds)
1   bottle (26 ounces) barbecue sauce
6   slices bacon
6   slices Swiss cheese

1. Place chicken in **CROCK-POT**® slow cooker. Cover with barbecue sauce. Cover; cook on LOW 8 to 9 hours. (If sauce becomes too thick during cooking, add a little water.)

2. Before serving, cut bacon slices in half. Cook bacon in microwave or on stove top, keeping bacon flat. Place 2 pieces cooked bacon on each chicken breast in **CROCK-POT**® slow cooker. Top with cheese. Cover; cook on HIGH until cheese melts.

*Tip: To make cleanup easier, coat the inside of the **CROCK-POT**® slow cooker with nonstick cooking spray before adding the ingredients. To remove any sticky barbecue sauce residue, soak the stoneware in hot sudsy water, then scrub it with a plastic or nylon scrubber; don't use steel wool.*

Caribbean Sweet Potato and Bean Stew

Makes 4 servings

2 medium sweet potatoes (about 1 pound), peeled and cut into 1-inch cubes
2 cups frozen cut green beans
1 can (15 ounces) black beans, rinsed and drained
1 can (14½ ounces) vegetable broth
1 small onion, sliced
2 teaspoons Caribbean jerk seasoning
½ teaspoon dried thyme
¼ teaspoon salt
¼ teaspoon ground cinnamon
⅓ cup slivered almonds, toasted*

To toast almonds, spread in single layer on baking sheet. Bake in preheated 350°F oven 8 to 10 minutes or until golden brown, stirring frequently.

Combine sweet potatoes, beans, broth, onion, jerk seasoning, thyme, salt and cinnamon in **CROCK-POT**® slow cooker. Cover; cook on LOW 5 to 6 hours or until vegetables are tender. Adjust seasonings. Serve with almonds.

Wild Mushroom Beef Stew

Makes 5 servings

1½	to 2 pounds beef stew meat, cut into 1-inch cubes
2	tablespoons all-purpose flour
½	teaspoon salt
½	teaspoon black pepper
1½	cups beef broth
1	teaspoon Worcestershire sauce
1	clove garlic, minced
1	bay leaf
1	teaspoon paprika
4	shiitake mushrooms,* sliced
2	medium carrots, sliced
2	medium red potatoes, diced
1	small white onion, chopped
1	rib celery, sliced

*If shiitake mushrooms are unavailable, substitute other mushrooms of your choice. For extra flavor, add a few dried porcini mushrooms.

1. Place beef in **CROCK-POT**® slow cooker. Mix together flour, salt and pepper; sprinkle over beef. Stir to coat each piece of beef with flour.

2. Add remaining ingredients and stir to mix well. Cover; cook on LOW 10 to 12 hours or on HIGH 4 to 6 hours. Stir stew before serving.

Tip: For 5-, 6-, or 7-quart **CROCK-POT**® slow cookers, double the amount of meat, mushrooms, carrots, potatoes, onion and celery.

Scalloped Potatoes and Ham

Makes 5 to 6 servings

    6   large russet potatoes, sliced into ¼-inch rounds
    1   ham steak (about 1½ pounds), cut into cubes
    1   can (10¾ ounces) condensed cream of mushroom soup, undiluted
    1   soup can water
    1   cup shredded Cheddar cheese
        Grill seasoning to taste

1. Layer potatoes and ham in **CROCK-POT®** slow cooker.

2. Combine soup, water, cheese and seasoning in large mixing bowl. Pour mixture over potatoes and ham. Cover; cook on HIGH 3½ hours or until potatoes are fork-tender. Turn **CROCK-POT®** slow cooker to LOW and continue cooking 1 hour.

Easy Beef Stew

Makes 4 to 6 servings

    2   pounds beef for stew, cut into 1-inch cubes
    1   can (4 ounces) mushrooms
    1   envelope (1 ounce) dry onion soup mix
    ⅓   cup red or white wine
    1   can (10 ounces) cream of mushroom soup, undiluted
        Hot cooked noodles

Combine all ingredients in **CROCK-POT®** slow cooker. Cover; cook on LOW 8 to 12 hours. Serve over noodles.

*Tip: Browning the beef before cooking it in the **CROCK-POT®** slow cooker isn't necessary but helps to enhance the flavor and appearance of the stew. If you have the time, use nonstick cooking spray and brown the meat in a large skillet before placing it in the stoneware; follow the recipe as written.*

Scalloped Potatoes and Ham

Three-Bean Turkey Chili

Makes 6 to 8 servings

- 1 **pound lean ground turkey**
- 1 **small onion, chopped**
- 1 **can (28 ounces) diced tomatoes, undrained**
- 1 **can (15 ounces) chickpeas, rinsed and drained**
- 1 **can (15 ounces) kidney beans, rinsed and drained**
- 1 **can (15 ounces) black beans, rinsed and drained**
- 1 **can (8 ounces) tomato sauce**
- 1 **can (4 ounces) diced mild green chilies**
- 1 **to 2 tablespoons chili powder**

1. Cook and stir turkey and onion in medium nonstick skillet over medium-high heat until turkey is no longer pink. Drain and discard fat. Transfer to **CROCK-POT®** slow cooker.

2. Add remaining ingredients; mix well. Cover; cook on HIGH 6 to 8 hours.

Three-Pepper Pasta Sauce

Makes 4 to 6 servings

1 each red, yellow and green bell pepper, cut into 1-inch pieces

2 cans (14½ ounces each) diced tomatoes, undrained

1 cup chopped onion

1 can (6 ounces) tomato paste

4 cloves garlic, minced

2 tablespoons olive oil

1 teaspoon dried basil

1 teaspoon dried oregano

½ teaspoon salt

¼ teaspoon red pepper flakes *or* black pepper

Hot cooked pasta

Shredded Parmesan or Romano cheese

1. Combine bell peppers, tomatoes with juice, onion, tomato paste, garlic, oil, basil, oregano, salt and pepper flakes in **CROCK-POT**® slow cooker. Cover; cook on LOW 7 to 8 hours or until vegetables are tender.

2. Adjust seasonings, if desired. Serve with pasta and cheese.

Tip: Save preparation time! Substitute 3 cups of mixed bell pepper chunks from a salad bar for the bell peppers.

Thai Chicken

Makes 6 servings

2½ pounds chicken pieces
1 cup hot salsa
¼ cup peanut butter
2 tablespoons lime juice
1 tablespoon soy sauce
1 teaspoon minced fresh ginger
Hot cooked rice
½ cup peanuts, chopped
2 tablespoons chopped fresh cilantro

1. Place chicken in **CROCK-POT**® slow cooker. Combine salsa, peanut butter, lime juice, soy sauce and ginger; pour over chicken.

2. Cover; cook on LOW 8 to 9 hours or on HIGH 3 to 4 hours, or until chicken is no longer pink in center.

3. Serve chicken and sauce over rice; sprinkle with peanuts and cilantro.

Tip: Cooking times are guidelines. Follow the recommended cooking times and keep the cover on your **CROCK-POT**® *slow cooker during the cooking process. At the end of the cooking time, check the internal temperature of poultry using an instant-read thermometer. Poultry should be at least 180°F.*

Kat's Slow Chicken

Makes 4 servings

4 to 6 **boneless skinless breasts** *or* 1 **cut-up whole chicken (3 pounds)**
1 jar (26 ounces) **spaghetti sauce**
1 medium **onion, sliced**
1 medium **green bell pepper, cut into strips**
4 **carrots, sliced**
1 rib **celery, sliced**
4 cloves **garlic, minced**
½ teaspoon **salt**
2 to 4 tablespoons **water, divided**
1 to 2 tablespoons **cornstarch**
Prepared mashed potatoes or hot cooked noodles (optional)

1. Combine chicken, sauce, onion, bell pepper, carrots, celery, garlic and salt in **CROCK-POT**® slow cooker. Cover; cook on LOW 6 to 8 hours.

2. Before serving, combine 2 tablespoons water and 1 tablespoon cornstarch in small bowl. Stir until mixture is smooth. Add to **CROCK-POT**® slow cooker. Cook on HIGH 15 minutes or until mixture thickens. If mixture needs additional thickening, add remaining water and cornstarch. Serve chicken and vegetables over mashed potatoes, if desired.

Tip: Vegetables such as potatoes and carrots can sometimes take longer to cook in a **CROCK-POT**® *slow cooker than meat. Place evenly cut vegetables along the sides of the* **CROCK-POT**® *slow cooker when possible.*

Chicken in Honey Sauce

Makes 6 servings

6 boneless skinless chicken breasts (about 1½ pounds)
Salt and black pepper, to taste
2 cups honey
1 cup soy sauce
½ cup ketchup
¼ cup oil
2 cloves garlic, minced
Sesame seeds

1. Place chicken in **CROCK-POT**® slow cooker; season with salt and pepper.

2. Combine honey, soy sauce, ketchup, oil and garlic in medium bowl. Pour over chicken. Cover; cook on LOW 6 to 8 hours or on HIGH 3 to 4 hours.

3. Garnish with sesame seeds before serving. Serve extra sauce on side, if desired.

*Tip: Recipes often provide a range of cooking times to account for variables, such as the temperature of the ingredients before cooking, the quantity of food in your **CROCK-POT**® slow cooker and the altitude; cooking times will be longer at higher altitudes.*

Chicken Sausage with Peppers & Basil

Makes 4 servings

1   tablespoon olive oil
1   clove garlic, minced
½   yellow onion, minced (about ½ cup)
1   pound sweet or hot Italian chicken sausage
1   can (28 ounces) whole tomatoes, drained and seeded
½   red bell pepper, cut into ½-inch slices
½   yellow bell pepper, cut into ½-inch slices
½   orange bell pepper, cut into ½-inch slices
¾   cup chopped fresh basil
     Crushed red pepper flakes, to taste
     Salt and black pepper, to taste
     Hot cooked pasta

1. Heat oil in large skillet over medium heat until hot. Add garlic and onion, and cook until translucent.

2. Remove sausage from casing and cut into 1-inch chunks. Add to skillet and cook 3 to 4 minutes, or until just beginning to brown. Transfer to **CROCK-POT**® slow cooker with slotted spoon, skimming off some fat.

3. Add tomatoes, bell peppers, basil, pepper flakes, salt and black pepper to **CROCK-POT**® slow cooker and stir to blend. Cook on HIGH 2½ to 3 hours, or until peppers have softened. Adjust seasonings to taste. Serve over pasta.

Tip: *It's not necessary to brown meat before slow cooking. However, if you prefer the look and flavor of browned meat, don't skip this step.*

Simple Shredded Pork Tacos

Makes 6 servings

2 pounds boneless pork roast

1 cup salsa

1 can (4 ounces) chopped green chilies

½ teaspoon garlic salt

½ teaspoon black pepper

Flour or corn tortillas

Optional toppings: salsa, sour cream, diced tomatoes, shredded cheese, shredded lettuce

1. Place roast, salsa, chilies, garlic salt and pepper in **CROCK-POT**® slow cooker. Cover; cook on LOW 8 hours, or until meat is tender.

2. Remove pork from **CROCK-POT**® slow cooker; shred with 2 forks. Serve on flour tortillas with sauce. Top as desired.

Mediterranean Chicken Breast and Wild Rice

Makes 4 servings

- 1 pound boneless skinless chicken breasts, lightly pounded
  Kosher salt, to taste
  Black pepper, to taste
- 1 cup wild-rice blend
- 10 cloves garlic, smashed
- ½ cup oil-packed or dry sun-dried tomatoes*
- ½ cup capers, drained
- 2 cups water
- ½ cup fresh-squeezed lemon juice
- ¼ cup extra-virgin olive oil

*If using dry sun-dried tomatoes, soak in boiling water to soften before chopping.

1. Season chicken with salt and black pepper. Place chicken in **CROCK-POT®** slow cooker. Add rice, garlic, tomatoes and capers; stir well.

2. Mix water, lemon juice and oil in small mixing bowl. Pour mixture over rice and chicken. Stir once to coat chicken. Cover; cook on LOW 8 hours.

Tip: Tapping or spinning the cover until the condensation falls off will allow you to see inside the **CROCK-POT®** slow cooker without removing the lid, which delays the cooking time.

Chicken Parisienne

Makes 6 servings

 6   boneless skinless chicken breasts (about 1½ pounds), cubed
½   teaspoon salt
½   teaspoon black pepper
½   teaspoon paprika
 1   can (10¾ ounces) condensed cream of mushroom *or* cream of chicken soup, undiluted
 2   cans (4 ounces each) sliced mushrooms, drained
½   cup dry white wine
 1   container (8 ounces) sour cream
    Hot cooked egg noodles

1. Place chicken in **CROCK-POT**® slow cooker. Sprinkle with salt, pepper and paprika. Add soup, mushrooms and wine; mix well. Cover; cook on HIGH 2 to 3 hours.

2. Add sour cream during last 30 minutes of cooking. Serve over noodles.

German-Style Bratwurst

Makes 6 to 8 servings

 4   pounds bratwurst
 2   pounds sauerkraut, drained
 6   apples, peeled, cored and thinly sliced
 1   white onion, thinly sliced
 1   teaspoon caraway seed
    Freshly ground black pepper
 5   bottles (12 ounces each) any German-style beer

Combine all ingredients in **CROCK-POT**® slow cooker. Cover; cook on LOW for 6 to 8 hours or on HIGH for 3 to 4 hours, or until done.

Chicken Stew

Makes 6 servings

- 4 **to 5 cups chopped cooked chicken**
- 1 **can (28 ounces) whole tomatoes, cut up, undrained**
- 2 **large red potatoes, cut into 1-inch pieces**
- 8 **ounces fresh okra, sliced**
- 1 **large onion, chopped**
- 1 **can (14 ounces) cream-style corn**
- ½ **cup ketchup**
- ½ **cup barbecue sauce**

Combine chicken, tomatoes with juice, potatoes, okra and onion in **CROCK-POT®** slow cooker. Cover; cook on LOW 6 to 8 hours or until potatoes are tender. Add corn, ketchup and barbecue sauce. Cover; cook on HIGH 30 minutes.

Slow Cooker Chicken and Rice

Makes 4 servings

- 3 **cans (10¾ ounces each) condensed cream of chicken soup, undiluted**
- 2 **cups uncooked instant rice**
- 1 **cup water**
- 1 **pound boneless skinless chicken breasts or chicken breast tenders**
- ½ **teaspoon salt**
- ¼ **teaspoon black pepper**
- ¼ **teaspoon paprika**
- ½ **cup diced celery**

Combine soup, rice and water in slow cooker. Add chicken; sprinkle with salt, pepper and paprika. Sprinkle celery over chicken. Cover; cook on LOW 6 to 8 hours or on HIGH 3 to 4 hours.

Korean Barbecue Beef

Makes 6 servings

4   to 4½ pounds beef short
    ribs
¼   cup chopped green onions
    with tops
¼   cup tamari or soy sauce
¼   cup beef broth or water
1   tablespoon brown sugar
2   teaspoons minced fresh
    ginger
2   teaspoons minced garlic
½   teaspoon black pepper
2   teaspoons dark sesame oil
    Hot cooked rice or linguini
    pasta
2   teaspoons sesame seeds,
    toasted

1. Place ribs in 5-quart **CROCK-POT**® slow cooker. Combine green onions, tamari, broth, brown sugar, ginger, garlic and pepper in medium bowl; mix well and pour over ribs. Cover; cook on LOW 7 to 8 hours or until ribs are fork-tender.

2. Remove ribs from cooking liquid. Cool slightly. Trim excess fat and discard. Cut rib meat into bite-size pieces, discarding bones and fat.

3. Let cooking liquid stand 5 minutes to allow fat to rise. Skim off fat and discard.

4. Stir sesame oil into cooking liquid. Return beef to **CROCK-POT**® slow cooker. Cover; cook 15 to 30 minutes or until hot. Serve over rice; garnish with sesame seeds.

Tip: *Three pounds of boneless short ribs can be substituted for the beef short ribs.*

Chinese Cashew Chicken

Makes 4 servings

- 1 can (16 ounces) bean sprouts, drained
- 2 cups sliced cooked chicken
- 1 can (10 ¾ ounces) condensed cream of mushroom soup, undiluted
- 1 cup sliced celery
- ½ cup chopped green onions with tops
- 1 can (4 ounces) sliced mushrooms, drained
- 3 tablespoons butter
- 1 tablespoon soy sauce
- 1 cup whole cashews
  Hot cooked rice

1. Combine bean sprouts, chicken, soup, celery, onions, mushrooms, butter and soy sauce in **CROCK-POT**® slow cooker; mix well. Cover; cook on LOW 4 to 6 hours or on HIGH 2 to 3 hours.

2. Stir in cashews just before serving. Serve over rice.

Tip: *For easier preparation, cut up the ingredients for this* **CROCK-POT**® *slow cooker recipe the night before. Don't place the* **CROCK-POT**® *stoneware in the refrigerator. Instead, wrap the chicken and vegetables separately, and store in the refrigerator.*

Cooking Across
America

Treat your family to regional favorites

Shrimp Jambalaya

Makes 6 servings

- 1 can (28 ounces) diced tomatoes, undrained
- 1 medium onion, chopped
- 1 medium red bell pepper, chopped
- 1 rib celery, chopped (about ½ cup)
- 2 tablespoons minced garlic
- 2 teaspoons dried parsley flakes
- 2 teaspoons dried oregano
- 1 teaspoon hot pepper sauce
- ½ teaspoon dried thyme
- 2 pounds cooked large shrimp
- 2 cups uncooked instant rice
- 2 cups fat-free reduced-sodium chicken broth

1. Combine tomatoes with juice, onion, bell pepper, celery, garlic, parsley, oregano, hot sauce and thyme in **CROCK-POT**® slow cooker. Cover; cook on LOW 8 hours or on HIGH 4 hours.

2. Stir in shrimp. Cover; cook on LOW 20 minutes.

3. Meanwhile, prepare rice according to package directions, substituting broth for water. Serve jambalaya over hot cooked rice.

Chicken Enchilada Roll-Ups

Makes 6 servings

- **6** **boneless skinless chicken breasts (about 1½ pounds)**
- **½** **cup plus 2 tablespoons all-purpose flour, divided**
- **½** **teaspoon salt**
- **2** **tablespoons butter**
- **1** **cup chicken broth**
- **1** **small onion, diced**
- **¼** **to ½ cup canned jalapeño peppers, sliced**
- **½** **teaspoon dried oregano**
- **2** **tablespoons heavy cream or milk**
- **6** **(7- to 8-inch) flour tortillas**
- **6** **thin slices American cheese *or* American cheese with jalapeño peppers**

1. Cut each chicken breast lengthwise into 2 or 3 strips. Combine ½ cup flour and salt in resealable plastic food storage bag. Add chicken strips and shake to coat with flour mixture. Melt butter in large skillet over medium heat. Brown chicken strips in batches, cooking 2 to 3 minutes per side. Transfer to **CROCK-POT®** slow cooker.

2. Add chicken broth to skillet and scrape up any browned bits. Pour broth mixture into **CROCK-POT®** slow cooker. Add onion, jalapeño peppers and oregano. Cover; cook on LOW 7 to 8 hours or on HIGH 3 to 4 hours.

3. Blend remaining 2 tablespoons flour and cream in small bowl until smooth. Stir into chicken mixture. Cook, uncovered, on HIGH 15 minutes or until thickened. Spoon chicken mixture onto center of flour tortillas. Top each with cheese slice. Fold up tortillas and serve.

Barbecued Pulled Pork

Makes 4 to 6 servings

- 1 **boneless pork shoulder or butt roast (3 to 4 pounds)**
- 1 **teaspoon salt**
- 1 **teaspoon ground cumin**
- 1 **teaspoon paprika**
- 1 **teaspoon black pepper**
- ½ **teaspoon ground red pepper**
- 1 **medium onion, thinly sliced**
- 1 **medium green bell pepper, cut into strips**
- 1 **bottle (18 ounces) barbecue sauce**
- ½ **cup packed light brown sugar Hot cooked rice or sandwich rolls**

1. Trim excess fat from pork and discard. Combine salt, cumin, paprika, black pepper and red pepper in small bowl; rub over roast.

2. Place onion and bell pepper in **CROCK-POT**® slow cooker; add pork. Combine barbecue sauce and sugar in medium bowl; pour over meat. Cover; cook on LOW 8 to 10 hours.

3. Remove roast from **CROCK-POT**® slow cooker. Trim and discard remaining fat from roast. Shred pork with 2 forks. Serve pork and sauce over rice.

*Tip: Don't add water to the **CROCK-POT**® slow cooker, unless the recipe specifically says to do so. Foods don't lose as much moisture during slow cooking as they can during conventional cooking, so follow the recipe guidelines for best results.*

Country Captain Chicken

Makes 4 servings

- **4 boneless skinless chicken thighs**
- **2 tablespoons all-purpose flour**
- **2 tablespoons vegetable oil, divided**
- **1 cup chopped green bell pepper**
- **1 large onion, chopped**
- **1 rib celery, chopped**
- **1 clove garlic, minced**
- **¼ cup chicken broth**
- **2 cups canned crushed tomatoes *or* diced fresh tomatoes**
- **½ cup golden raisins**
- **1½ teaspoons curry powder**
- **1 teaspoon salt**
- **¼ teaspoon paprika**
- **¼ teaspoon black pepper**
- **Hot cooked rice**
- **Parsley (optional)**

1. Coat chicken with flour; set aside. Heat 1 tablespoon oil in large skillet over medium-high heat until hot. Add bell pepper, onion, celery and garlic. Cook and stir 5 minutes or until vegetables are tender. Place vegetables in **CROCK-POT**® slow cooker.

2. Heat remaining 1 tablespoon oil in same skillet over medium-high heat. Add chicken; cook 5 minutes per side or until browned. Place chicken in **CROCK-POT**® slow cooker.

3. Pour broth into skillet. Cook and stir over medium-high heat, scraping up any browned bits from bottom of skillet. Pour broth mixture into **CROCK-POT**® slow cooker. Add tomatoes, raisins, curry powder, salt, paprika and black pepper. Cover; cook on LOW 3 hours. Serve chicken and sauce over rice. Garnish with parsley, if desired.

Wisconsin Beer and Cheese Soup

Makes 4 servings

- 2 to 3 slices pumpernickel or rye bread
- 1 can (14½ ounces) chicken broth
- 1 cup beer
- ¼ cup finely chopped onion
- 2 cloves garlic, minced
- ¾ teaspoon dried thyme
- 6 ounces American cheese, shredded or diced
- 4 to 6 ounces sharp Cheddar cheese, shredded
- 1 cup milk
- ½ teaspoon paprika

1. Preheat oven to 425°F. Slice bread into ½-inch cubes; place on baking sheet. Bake 10 to 12 minutes, or until crisp, stirring once; set aside.

2. Combine broth, beer, onion, garlic and thyme in **CROCK-POT**® slow cooker. Cover; cook on LOW 4 hours.

3. Turn **CROCK-POT**® slow cooker to HIGH. Stir in cheeses, milk and paprika. Cover; cook 45 minutes to 1 hour, or until soup is hot and cheeses are melted. Stir soup well to blend cheeses. Ladle soup into bowls; top with croutons.

Tip: *Choose a light-tasting beer when making this soup. Hearty ales have a stronger flavor that might not please your family's taste buds.*

Hot and Juicy Reuben Sandwiches

Makes 4 servings

- 1 mild-cure corned beef (about 1½ pounds)
- 2 cups sauerkraut, drained
- ½ cup beef broth
- 1 small onion, sliced
- 1 clove garlic, minced
- ¼ teaspoon caraway seeds
- 4 to 6 peppercorns
- 8 slices pumpernickel or rye bread
- 4 slices Swiss cheese
  Mustard

1. Trim excess fat from corned beef. Place meat in the **CROCK-POT**® slow cooker. Add sauerkraut, broth, onion, garlic, caraway seeds andpeppercorns. Cover; cook on LOW 7 to 9 hours.

2. Remove beef from **CROCK-POT**® slow cooker. Cut beef across grain into 4 (½-inch-thick) slices. Divide evenly among 4 slices of bread. Top each slice with ½ cup drained sauerkraut mixture and 1 slice cheese. Spread mustard on remaining 4 bread slices, and place on sandwiches.

Fall-Apart Pork Roast with Mole

Makes 6 servings

⅔ cup whole almonds

⅔ cup raisins

3 tablespoons oil, divided

½ cup chopped onion

4 cloves garlic, chopped

2¾ pounds lean boneless pork shoulder roast, well trimmed

1 can (14½ ounces) diced fire-roasted tomatoes *or* diced tomatoes, undrained

1 cup cubed bread, any type

½ cup chicken broth

2 ounces Mexican chocolate, chopped

2 tablespoons chipotle peppers in adobo sauce, chopped

1 teaspoon salt

Fresh cilantro, coarsely chopped (optional)

1. Heat large skillet over medium-high heat. Add almonds and toast 3 to 4 minutes, stirring frequently, until fragrant. Add raisins. Cook 1 to 2 minutes longer, stirring constantly, until raisins begin to plump. Place half of almond mixture in large mixing bowl. Reserve remaining half for garnish.

2. In same skillet, heat 1 tablespoon oil. Add onions and garlic. Cook 2 to 3 minutes, stirring constantly, until softened. Add to almond mixture; set aside.

3. Heat remaining oil in same skillet. Add pork roast and brown on all sides, about 5 to 7 minutes. Place pork roast in **CROCK-POT**® slow cooker.

4. Combine tomatoes with juice, bread, broth, chocolate, chipotle peppers and salt with almond-onion mixture. Process mixture in blender, in 2 or 3 batches, until smooth. Pour mixture over pork.

5. Cover; cook on LOW 7 to 8 hours or on HIGH 3 to 4 hours or until pork is done. Remove pork roast from **CROCK-POT**® slow cooker. Whisk sauce in slow cooker and spoon over roast. Garnish with reserved almond mixture and chopped cilantro, if desired.

Southwestern Corn and Beans

Makes 6 servings

1 tablespoon olive oil
1 large onion, diced
1 or 2 jalapeño peppers,* diced
1 clove garlic, minced
2 cans (15 ounces each) light red kidney beans, rinsed and drained
1 bag (16 ounces) frozen corn, thawed
1 can (14½ ounces) diced tomatoes, undrained
1 green bell pepper, cut into 1-inch pieces
2 teaspoons medium-hot chili powder
¾ teaspoon salt
½ teaspoon ground cumin
½ teaspoon black pepper
Sour cream or plain yogurt (optional)
Sliced black olives (optional)

*Jalapeño peppers can sting and irritate the skin; wear rubber gloves when handling peppers and do not touch eyes. Wash hands after handling.

1. Heat oil in medium skillet over medium heat. Add onion, jalapeño pepper and garlic; cook 5 minutes. Combine onion mixture, beans, corn, tomatoes with juice, bell pepper, chili powder, salt, cumin and black pepper in **CROCK-POT**® slow cooker; mix well. Cover; cook on LOW 7 to 8 hours or on HIGH 2 to 3 hours.

2. Serve with sour cream and black olives, if desired.

Tip: For a party, spoon this colorful vegetarian dish into hollowed-out bell peppers or bread bowls.

Burgundy Beef Po' Boys with Dipping Sauce

Makes 6 to 8 sandwiches

- 1 boneless beef chuck shoulder or bottom round roast (3 pounds)
- 2 cups chopped onions
- ¼ cup dry red wine
- 3 tablespoons balsamic vinegar
- 1 tablespoon beef bouillon granules
- 1 tablespoon Worcestershire sauce
- ¾ teaspoon dried thyme
- ½ teaspoon garlic powder
  Italian rolls, warmed and split

1. Trim excess fat from beef and discard. Cut beef into 3 or 4 pieces. Place onions on bottom of **CROCK-POT**® slow cooker. Top with beef and remaining ingredients, except rolls. Cover; cook on HIGH 8 to 10 hours or until beef is very tender.

2. Remove beef from **CROCK-POT**® slow cooker; cool slightly. Trim excess fat and discard. Shred with 2 forks. Let cooking liquid stand 5 minutes to allow fat to rise. Skim off fat and discard. Spoon beef into rolls. Serve cooking liquid as dipping sauce.

Creole Vegetables and Chicken

Makes 8 servings

1   can (14½ ounces) no-salt-added diced tomatoes, undrained
8   ounces frozen cut okra
2   cups chopped green bell pepper
1   cup chopped yellow onion
¾   cup sliced celery
1   cup low-sodium fat-free chicken broth
2   teaspoons Worcestershire sauce
1   teaspoon dried thyme
1   bay leaf
1   pound chicken tenders, cut into bite-size pieces
¾   teaspoon Creole seasoning
1½ teaspoons sugar
1   tablespoon extra-virgin olive oil
    Hot pepper sauce, to taste
¼   cup chopped parsley

1. Coat **CROCK-POT**® slow cooker with cooking spray. Add tomatoes with juice, okra, bell pepper, onion, celery, broth, Worcestershire sauce, thyme and bay leaf. Cover; cook on LOW 9 hours or on HIGH 4½ hours.

2. Coat medium nonstick skillet with cooking spray. Heat over medium-high heat until hot. Add chicken; cook and stir 6 minutes or until beginning to lightly brown. Transfer chicken to **CROCK-POT**® slow cooker. Add remaining ingredients, except parsley, and cook on HIGH 15 minutes to blend flavors. Stir in parsley.

Tip: To slightly thicken stews in the CROCK-POT® slow cooker, remove the solid foods and leave the cooking liquid in the stoneware. Mix 2 to 4 tablespoons cornstarch with ¼ cup cold water until smooth. Stir this mixture into the CROCK-POT® slow cooker and cook on HIGH until the mixture is smooth.

Southwestern Stuffed Peppers

Makes 4 servings

4 green bell peppers

1 can (15 ounces) black beans, rinsed and drained

1 cup (4 ounces) shredded pepper-jack cheese

¾ cup medium salsa

½ cup frozen corn

½ cup chopped green onions with tops

⅓ cup uncooked long-grain white rice

1 teaspoon chili powder

½ teaspoon ground cumin

Sour cream (optional)

1. Cut thin slice off top of each bell pepper. Carefully remove seeds and membrane, leaving pepper whole.

2. Combine beans, cheese, salsa, corn, onions, rice, chili powder and cumin in medium bowl. Spoon filling evenly into each pepper. Place peppers in **CROCK-POT**® slow cooker.

3. Cover; cook on LOW 4 to 6 hours. Serve with sour cream, if desired.

Tip: *If you prefer firmer rice when your dish is finished, substitute converted rice for regular long-grain white rice.*

Sauerkraut Pork Ribs

Makes 12 servings

- 1 tablespoon oil
- 3 to 4 pounds pork country-style ribs
- 1 large onion, thinly sliced
- 1 teaspoon caraway seeds
- ½ teaspoon garlic powder
- ¼ to ½ teaspoon black pepper
- ¾ cup water
- 2 jars (about 28 ounces each) sauerkraut
- 12 medium red potatoes, quartered

1. Heat oil in large skillet over medium-low heat until hot. Brown ribs on all sides. Transfer to **CROCK-POT**® slow cooker. Drain excess fat and discard.

2. Add onion to skillet; cook until tender. Add caraway seeds, garlic powder and pepper; cook 15 minutes. Transfer onion mixture to **CROCK-POT**® slow cooker.

3. Add water to skillet and scrape up any brown bits. Pour pan juices into **CROCK-POT**® slow cooker. Partially drain sauerkraut, leaving some liquid; pour over meat. Top with potatoes. Cover; cook on LOW 6 to 8 hours or until potatoes are tender, stirring once during cooking.

Cajun Chicken and Shrimp Creole

Makes 6 servings

- 1 pound boneless skinless chicken thighs
- 1 red bell pepper, chopped
- 1 large onion, chopped
- 1 rib celery, diced
- 1 can (15 ounces) stewed tomatoes, undrained and chopped
- 1 clove garlic, minced
- 1 tablespoon sugar
- 1 teaspoon paprika
- 1 teaspoon Cajun seasoning
- 1 teaspoon salt
- 1 teaspoon black pepper
- 1 pound shrimp, peeled, deveined and cleaned
- 1 tablespoon fresh lemon juice

Louisiana-style hot sauce, to taste

Hot cooked rice

1. Place chicken thighs in **CROCK-POT®** slow cooker. Add bell pepper, onion, celery, tomatoes with juice, garlic, sugar, paprika, Cajun seasoning, salt and pepper. Cover; cook on LOW 7 to 9 hours or on HIGH 3 to 4 hours.

2. Add shrimp, lemon juice and hot sauce. Cover; cook on LOW 45 minutes to 1 hour or until shrimp are done. Serve over hot rice.

*Tip: For 5-, 6-, or 7-quart **CROCK-POT®** slow cookers, double all ingredients.*

Philly Cheese Steaks

Makes 8 servings

- 2 pounds round steak, sliced
- 2 tablespoons butter or margarine, melted
- 4 onions, sliced
- 2 green bell peppers, sliced
- 1 tablespoon garlic-pepper blend
  Salt, to taste
- ½ cup water
- 2 teaspoons beef bouillon granules
- 8 crusty Italian or French rolls,* sliced in half
- 8 slices Cheddar cheese, cut in half

   *Toast rolls on griddle or under broiler, if desired.

1. Combine steak, butter, onions, bell peppers, garlic-pepper blend and salt in **CROCK-POT**® slow cooker; stir to mix.

2. Whisk together water and bouillon in small bowl; pour into **CROCK-POT**® slow cooker. Cover; cook on LOW 6 to 8 hours.

3. Remove meat, onions and bell peppers from **CROCK-POT**® slow cooker and pile on rolls. Top beef with cheese and place under broiler until cheese is melted.

Beyond Basic
Soups

Slow-simmer flavorful varieties

Chicken Tortilla Soup

Makes 4 to 6 servings

4   boneless skinless chicken thighs (about 1 pound)
2   cans (15 ounces each) diced tomatoes, undrained
1   can (4 ounces) chopped mild green chilies, drained
1   yellow onion, diced
2   cloves garlic, minced
½   to 1 cup chicken broth
1   teaspoon cumin
    Salt and black pepper, to taste
4   corn tortillas, sliced into ¼-inch strips
2   tablespoons chopped fresh cilantro
½   cup shredded Monterey Jack cheese
1   avocado, seeded, peeled, diced and tossed with lime juice to prevent browning
    Lime wedges

1. Place chicken in **CROCK-POT**® slow cooker. Combine tomatoes with juice, chilies, onion, garlic, ½ cup chicken broth and cumin in small bowl. Pour mixture over chicken. Cover; cook on HIGH 3 hours, or until chicken is tender.

2. Remove chicken from **CROCK-POT**® slow cooker. Shred with 2 forks. Return to cooking liquid. Adjust seasonings, adding more broth if necessary.

3. Just before serving, add tortillas and cilantro to **CROCK-POT**® slow cooker. Stir to blend. Serve in soup bowls, topping each serving with cheese, avocado and a squeeze of lime juice.

Roast Tomato-Basil Soup

Makes 6 servings

2   **cans (28 ounces each) peeled whole tomatoes, drained and 3 cups liquid reserved**

2½   **tablespoons packed dark brown sugar**

1   **medium onion, finely chopped**

3   **cups chicken broth**

3   **tablespoons tomato paste**

¼   **teaspoon ground allspice**

1   **can (5 ounces) evaporated milk**

¼   **cup shredded fresh basil (about 10 large leaves)**

    Salt and black pepper, to taste

1. Preheat oven to 450°F. Line baking sheet with foil; spray with nonstick cooking spray. Arrange tomatoes on foil in single layer. Sprinkle with brown sugar and top with onion. Bake about 25 to 30 minutes or until tomatoes look dry and light brown. Let tomatoes cool slightly; finely chop.

2. Place tomato mixture, 3 cups reserved liquid from tomatoes, broth, tomato paste and allspice in **CROCK-POT®** slow cooker. Mix well. Cover; cook on LOW 8 hours or on HIGH 4 hours.

3. Add evaporated milk and basil; season with salt and pepper. Cook on HIGH 30 minutes or until hot.

Vegetable and Red Lentil Soup

Makes 4 servings

- 1 can (14½ ounces) vegetable broth
- 1 can (14½ ounces) diced tomatoes, undrained
- 2 medium zucchini or yellow summer squash (or 1 of each), diced
- 1 red or yellow bell pepper, diced
- ½ cup thinly sliced carrots
- ½ cup red lentils, rinsed and sorted*
- ½ teaspoon salt
- ½ teaspoon sugar
- ¼ teaspoon black pepper
- 2 tablespoons chopped fresh basil *or* thyme
- ½ cup croutons or shredded cheese (optional)

*If you have difficulty finding red lentils, substitute brown lentils instead.

1. Combine broth, tomatoes with juice, zucchini, bell pepper, carrots, lentils, salt, sugar and black pepper in **CROCK-POT**® slow cooker; mix well. Cover; cook on LOW 8 hours or on HIGH 4 hours, or until lentils and vegetables are tender.

2. Ladle into shallow bowls. Sprinkle on basil and croutons, if desired.

Tip: *When adapting your favorite recipe for a **CROCK-POT**® slow cooker, reduce the liquid by as much as half, because foods don't lose as much moisture during slow cooking as they can during conventional cooking.*

Cioppino

Makes 6 servings

- 1 pound cod, halibut, or any firm-fleshed white fish, cubed
- 1 cup mushrooms, sliced
- 2 carrots, sliced
- 1 onion, chopped
- 1 green bell pepper, chopped
- 1 teaspoon minced garlic
- 1 can (15 ounces) tomato sauce
- 1 can (14 ounces) beef broth
- 1 teaspoon salt
- ½ teaspoon black pepper
- ½ teaspoon dried oregano
- 1 can (7 ounces) cooked clams
- ½ pound cooked shrimp
- 1 package (6 ounces) cooked crabmeat
  Minced parsley

1. Combine fish pieces, mushrooms, carrots, onion, bell pepper, garlic, tomato sauce, broth, salt, black pepper and oregano in **CROCK-POT**® slow cooker. Cover; cook on LOW 10 to 12 hours.

2. Turn **CROCK-POT**® slow cooker to HIGH. Add clams, shrimp and crabmeat. Cover; cook 15 to 30 minutes or until seafood is heated through. Garnish with parsley before serving.

*Tip: Shellfish and mollusks are delicate and should be added to the **CROCK-POT**® slow cooker during the last 15 to 30 minutes of the cooking time if you're using the HIGH heat setting, and during the last 30 to 45 minutes if you're using the LOW setting. This type of seafood overcooks easily, becoming tough and rubbery, so watch your cooking times, and cook only long enough for foods to be done.*

Mushroom Barley Stew

Makes 4 to 6 servings

1 **tablespoon olive oil**
1 **medium onion, finely chopped**
1 **cup chopped carrots (about 2 carrots)**
1 **clove garlic, minced**
1 **cup uncooked pearl barley**
1 **cup dried wild mushrooms, broken into pieces**
1 **teaspoon salt**
½ **teaspoon black pepper**
½ **teaspoon dried thyme**
5 **cups vegetable broth**

1. Heat oil in medium skillet over medium-high heat. Add onion, carrots and garlic; cook and stir 5 minutes or until tender. Place in **CROCK-POT**® slow cooker.

2. Add barley, mushrooms, salt, pepper and thyme. Stir in broth. Cover; cook on LOW 6 to 7 hours. Adjust seasonings.

Tip: To turn this thick robust stew into a soup, add 2 to 3 additional cups of broth. Cook the same length of time.

Chicken and Sweet Potato Stew

Makes 6 servings

- 4 boneless skinless chicken breasts, cut into bite-size pieces
- 2 medium sweet potatoes, peeled and cubed
- 2 medium Yukon Gold potatoes, peeled and cubed
- 2 medium carrots, peeled and cut into ½-inch slices
- 1 can (28 ounces) whole stewed tomatoes, undrained
- 1 teaspoon salt
- 1 teaspoon paprika
- 1 teaspoon celery seeds
- ½ teaspoon black pepper
- ⅛ teaspoon ground cinnamon
- ⅛ teaspoon ground nutmeg
- 1 cup fat-free low-sodium chicken broth
- ¼ cup fresh basil, chopped

Combine chicken, potatoes, carrots, tomatoes with juice, salt, paprika, celery seeds, pepper, cinnamon, nutmeg and broth in the **CROCK-POT**® slow cooker. Cover; cook on LOW 6 to 8 hours or on HIGH 3 to 4 hours. To serve, sprinkle with basil.

Tip: For 5-, 6-, or 7-quart **CROCK-POT**® slow cookers, double all ingredients.

Manhattan Clam Chowder

Makes 4 servings

3   slices bacon, diced
2   celery stalks, chopped
3   onions, chopped
2   cups water
1   can (15 ounces) stewed tomatoes, undrained and chopped
4   small red potatoes, diced
2   carrots, diced
½   teaspoon dried thyme
½   teaspoon black pepper
½   teaspoon Louisiana-style hot sauce
1   pound minced clams*

*If minced clams are unavailable, use canned clams; 6 (6½-ounce) cans yield about 1 pound of clam meat; drain and discard liquid.

1. Cook and stir bacon in medium saucepan until bacon is crisp. Remove bacon and place in **CROCK-POT®** slow cooker.

2. Add celery and onions to skillet. Cook and stir until tender. Place in **CROCK-POT®** slow cooker.

3. Mix in water, tomatoes with juice, potatoes, carrots, thyme, pepper and hot sauce. Cover; cook on LOW 6 to 8 hours or HIGH 4 to 6 hours. Add clams during last hour of cooking.

Tip: Shellfish and mollusks are delicate and should be added to the **CROCK-POT®** slow cooker during the last 15 to 30 minutes of the cooking time if you're using the HIGH heat setting, and during the last 30 to 45 minutes if you're using the LOW setting. This type of seafood overcooks easily, becoming tough and rubbery, so watch your cooking times, and cook only long enough for foods to be done.

Easy Corn Chowder

Makes 6 servings

2   cans (14½ ounces each) chicken broth
1   bag (16 ounces) frozen whole kernel corn, thawed
3   small red potatoes, peeled and cut into ½-inch pieces
1   red bell pepper, diced
1   medium onion, diced
1   rib celery, sliced
½   teaspoon salt
½   teaspoon black pepper
¼   teaspoon ground coriander
½   cup heavy cream
8   slices bacon, crisp-cooked and crumbled

1. Place broth, corn, potatoes, bell pepper, onion, celery, salt, black pepper and coriander into **CROCK-POT**® slow cooker. Cover; cook on LOW 7 to 8 hours.

2. Partially mash soup mixture with potato masher to thicken. Stir in cream; cook on HIGH, uncovered, until hot. Adjust seasonings, if desired. To serve, sprinkle on bacon.

Tip: Defrost meat and vegetables before cooking them in the **CROCK-POT**® slow cooker.

Chicken Fiesta Soup

Makes 8 servings

- 4 boneless skinless chicken breasts, cooked and shredded
- 1 can (14½ ounces) stewed tomatoes, drained
- 2 cans (4 ounces each) chopped green chilies
- 1 can (28 ounces) enchilada sauce
- 1 can (14½ ounces) chicken broth
- 1 cup finely chopped onion
- 2 cloves garlic, minced
- 1 teaspoon salt
- 1 teaspoon ground cumin
- 1 teaspoon chili powder
- ¾ teaspoon black pepper
- ¼ cup minced fresh cilantro
- 1 cup frozen whole kernel corn
- 1 yellow squash, diced
- 1 zucchini, diced
- 8 tostada shells, crumbled
- 8 ounces shredded Cheddar cheese

1. Combine chicken, tomatoes, chilies, enchilada sauce, broth, onions, garlic, salt, cumin, chili powder, pepper, cilantro, corn, squash and zucchini in **CROCK-POT**® slow cooker. Cover; cook on LOW for 8 hours.

2. To serve, fill individual bowls with soup. Garnish with crumbled tostada shells and cheese.

*Tip: The flavor and aroma of crushed or ground herbs and spices may lessen during a longer cooking time. So, for slow cooking in your **CROCK-POT**® slow cooker, you may use whole herbs and spices. Be sure to taste and adjust your seasonings before serving.*

New England Clam Chowder

Makes 6 to 8 servings

6   slices bacon, diced
2   onions, chopped
5   cans (6½ ounces each) clams, drained and liquid reserved
6   medium red potatoes, cubed
2   tablespoons minced garlic
1   teaspoon black pepper
2   cans (12 ounces each) evaporated milk
    Salt, to taste

1. Cook and stir bacon and onion in medium skillet until onions are tender. Place in **CROCK-POT**® slow cooker.

2. Add enough water to reserved clam liquid to make 3 cups. Pour into **CROCK-POT**® slow cooker, and add potatoes, garlic and pepper. Cover; cook on LOW 5 to 8 hours or HIGH 1 to 3 hours.

3. Turn **CROCK-POT**® slow cooker to LOW and mix in reserved clams and milk. Cover; cook 1 hour. Adjust seasoning, if necessary.

*Tip: Shellfish and mollusks are delicate and should be added to the **CROCK-POT**® slow cooker during the last 15 to 30 minutes of the cooking time if you're using the HIGH heat setting, and during the last 30 to 45 minutes if you're using the LOW setting. This type of seafood overcooks easily, becoming tough and rubbery, so watch your cooking times, and cook only long enough for foods to be done.*

Thai-Style Chicken Pumpkin Soup

Makes 4 to 6 servings

1	tablespoon extra-virgin olive oil
6	boneless skinless chicken breasts, cut into 1-inch cubes
1	large white onion, thinly sliced
3	cloves garlic, minced
1	tablespoon minced fresh ginger
½	to ¾ teaspoon crushed red pepper flakes
2	stalks celery, trimmed and diced
2	carrots, peeled, trimmed and diced
1	can (15 ounces) solid-pack pumpkin
½	cup mango nectar
½	cup fresh lime juice
½	cup creamy peanut butter
4	cups low-sodium chicken broth
3	tablespoons rice vinegar
½	cup minced fresh cilantro, divided
½	cup heavy cream
1	tablespoon cornstarch
2	to 4 cups hot cooked rice (preferably jasmine or basmati)
3	green onions, minced
½	cup roasted unsalted peanuts, coarsely chopped
	Lime wedges (optional)

1. Heat oil in large nonstick skillet over medium heat. Add chicken and cook, stirring occasionally, about 3 minutes. Add onion, garlic, ginger and red pepper flakes; cook for 1 or 2 minutes longer or until mixture is fragrant.

2. Transfer chicken mixture to **CROCK-POT**® slow cooker. Add celery, carrots, pumpkin, mango nectar, lime juice, peanut butter, broth and 2 cups water; stir to combine. Cover; cook on LOW 8 hours or on HIGH 4 hours.

3. Stir in rice vinegar and ¼ cup cilantro. Mix cream and cornstarch together in small mixing bowl. Stir mixture into soup. Turn setting to HIGH. Simmer, uncovered, 10 minutes or until soup thickens.

4. To serve, put rice in soup bowls. Ladle soup around rice. Sprinkle with remaining cilantro, green onion and peanuts. Squeeze fresh lime juice over soup, if desired.

Parsnip and Carrot Soup

Makes 4 servings

- 1 medium leek, thinly sliced
- 4 medium parsnips, peeled and diced
- 4 medium carrots, peeled and diced
- 4 cups fat-free chicken broth
- 1 bay leaf
- ½ teaspoon salt
- ½ teaspoon black pepper
- ½ cup small pasta, cooked al denté and drained
- 1 cup low-fat croutons
- 1 tablespoon chopped Italian parsley

1. Coat small skillet with nonstick cooking spray. Heat over medium heat until hot. Cook and stir leek until golden. Transfer to **CROCKPOT**® slow cooker.

2. Add parsnips, carrots, broth, bay leaf, salt and pepper. Cover; cook on LOW 6 to 9 hours or on HIGH 2 to 4 hours, or until vegetables are tender.

3. Add pasta during the last hour of cooking. Remove bay leaf before serving. Garnish with croutons and parsley.

Tip: *For 5-, 6-, or 7-quart* **CROCK-POT**® *slow cookers, double all ingredients.*

Curried Butternut Squash Soup

Makes 6 to 8 servings

2 pounds butternut squash, rinsed, peeled, seeded and chopped into 1-inch cubes
1 firm crisp apple, peeled, seeded and chopped
1 yellow onion, chopped
5 cups chicken stock
1 tablespoon curry powder, sweet or hot
¼ teaspoon ground cloves
   Salt and black pepper, to taste
¼ cup chopped dried cranberries (optional)

1. Place squash, apple and onion into **CROCK-POT**® slow cooker.

2. Mix together stock, curry powder and cloves in small bowl. Pour mixture into **CROCK-POT**® slow cooker. Cover; cook on LOW 5 to 5½ hours or on HIGH 4 hours, or until vegetables are tender.

3. Process in blender, in 2 or 3 batches, to desired consistency. Add salt and black pepper. Garnish with cranberries, if desired.

Black Bean Chipotle Soup

Makes 4 to 6 servings

1   **pound dry black beans**
2   **stalks celery, cut into ¼-inch dice**
2   **carrots, cut into ¼-inch dice**
1   **yellow onion, cut into ¼-inch dice**
2   **chipotle peppers in adobo sauce, chopped***
1   **cup crushed tomatoes**
1   **can (4 ounces) chopped mild green chilies, drained**
6   **cups chicken or vegetable stock**
2   **teaspoons cumin**
     Salt and black pepper, to taste
     Optional toppings: sour cream, chunky-style salsa, fresh chopped cilantro

*If using dried chipotles, soak in warm water to soften before chopping, about 20 minutes.

1. Rinse and sort beans and place in large bowl; cover completely with water. Soak 6 to 8 hours or overnight. (To quick-soak beans, place beans in large saucepan; cover with water. Bring to a boil over high heat. Boil 2 minutes. Remove from heat; let soak, covered, 1 hour.) Drain beans; discard water.

2. Place beans in **CROCK-POT®** slow cooker. Add celery, carrots and onion.

3. Combine chipotles, tomatoes, chilies, stock and cumin in medium bowl. Add to **CROCK-POT®** slow cooker. Cover; cook on LOW 7 to 8 hours or on HIGH 4½ to 5 hours, or until beans are tender. Season with salt and pepper.

4. If desired, process mixture in blender, in 2 or 3 batches, to desired consistency, or leave chunky. Serve with sour cream, salsa and cilantro, if desired.

Tip: *For an even heartier soup, add 1 cup diced browned spicy sausage, such as linguica or chourico.*

Simmering Hot and Sour Soup

Makes 4 servings

- 2 cans (14½ ounces each) chicken broth
- 1 cup chopped cooked chicken or pork
- 4 ounces fresh shiitake mushroom caps, thinly sliced
- ½ cup sliced bamboo shoots, cut into thin strips
- 3 tablespoons rice wine vinegar
- 2 tablespoons soy sauce
- 1½ teaspoons chili paste *or* 1 teaspoon hot chili oil
- 4 ounces firm tofu, well drained and cut into ½-inch pieces
- 2 teaspoons sesame oil
- 2 tablespoons cornstarch
- 2 tablespoons cold water
  Chopped cilantro *or* sliced green onions

1. Combine broth, chicken, mushrooms, bamboo shoots, vinegar, soy sauce and chili paste in **CROCK-POT**® slow cooker. Cover; cook on LOW 3 to 4 hours or on HIGH 2 to 3 hours, or until done.

2. Stir in tofu and sesame oil. Combine cornstarch with water; mix well. Add to soup and mix in well. Cover; cook on HIGH 10 minutes or until soup has thickened. To serve, sprinkle on cilantro.

Weeknight
Winners

Don't wait for Sunday to serve great meals

Chicken Provençal

Makes 8 servings

2 pounds boneless skinless chicken thighs, each cut into quarters
2 medium red peppers, cut into ¼-inch-thick slices
1 medium yellow pepper, cut into ¼-inch-thick slices
1 onion, thinly sliced
1 can (28 ounces) plum tomatoes, drained
3 cloves garlic, minced
¼ teaspoon salt
¼ teaspoon dried thyme
¼ teaspoon fennel seeds, crushed
3 strips orange peel
½ cup fresh basil, chopped

1. Place chicken, bell peppers, onion, tomatoes, garlic, salt, thyme, fennel seeds and orange peel in **CROCK-POT®** slow cooker. Mix thoroughly. Cover; cook on LOW 7 to 9 hours or on HIGH 3 to 4 hours.

2. To serve, sprinkle with basil.

Tip: *For 5-, 6-, or 7-quart* **CROCK-POT®** *slow cookers, double all ingredients.*

Chunky Chili

Makes 4 servings

- 1 pound 90% lean ground beef
- 1 medium onion, chopped
- 2 cans (14½ ounces each) diced tomatoes, undrained
- 1 can (15 ounces) pinto beans, rinsed and drained
- ½ cup prepared salsa
- 1 tablespoon chili powder
- 1½ teaspoons ground cumin
  Salt and black pepper, to taste
- ½ cup (2 ounces) shredded Cheddar cheese
- ¼ cup diced onions
- 4 teaspoons sliced black olives

1. Cook and stir beef and onion in large skillet at medium-high heat until beef is browned and onion is tender. Drain and discard fat.

2. Place beef mixture, tomatoes with juice, beans, salsa, chili powder and cumin in **CROCK-POT**® slow cooker; stir. Cover; cook on LOW 5 to 6 hours or until flavors are blended. Season with salt and pepper. Serve with cheese, onions and olives.

Tip: Tapping or spinning the cover until the condensation falls off will allow you to see inside the **CROCK-POT**® slow cooker without removing the lid, which delays the cooking time.

Hearty Beef Short Ribs

Makes 6 to 8 servings

2½   pounds beef short ribs, bone-in
1   to 2 tablespoons coarse salt
1   to 2 tablespoons black pepper
2   tablespoons olive oil, divided
2   carrots, cut into ¼-inch dice
2   celery stalks, cut into ¼-inch dice
1   large yellow onion, cut into ¼-inch dice
3   cloves garlic, minced
3   bay leaves
⅓   cup red wine
⅓   cup crushed tomatoes
⅓   cup balsamic vinegar

1. Season ribs with salt and black pepper. Drizzle with 1 tablespoon olive oil. Heat 1 tablespoon olive oil in large skillet. Cook ribs until just browned, about 2 to 3 minutes per side. Transfer ribs to **CROCK-POT**® slow cooker. Add carrots, celery, onion, garlic and bay leaves.

2. Combine wine, tomatoes and vinegar in small bowl. Season with salt and black pepper, if desired. Pour mixture into **CROCK-POT**® slow cooker. Cover; cook on LOW 8 to 9 hours or HIGH 5½ to 6 hours, turning once or twice, until meat is tender and falling off the bone.

3. Remove ribs from **CROCK-POT**® slow cooker. Process sauce in blender to desired consistency. To serve, pour sauce over ribs.

Tip: *To make cleanup easier, spray the inside of the **CROCK-POT**® slow cooker with nonstick cooking spray before adding the food.*

Cream Cheese Chicken with Broccoli

Makes 10 to 12 servings

4 pounds boneless skinless chicken breasts, cut into ½-inch pieces
1 tablespoon olive oil
1 package (1 ounce) Italian salad dressing mix
2 cups sliced mushrooms
1 cup chopped onion
1 can (10¾ ounces) condensed low-fat cream of chicken soup, undiluted
1 bag (10 ounces) frozen broccoli florets, thawed
1 package (8 ounces) low-fat cream cheese, cubed
¼ cup dry sherry
   Hot cooked pasta

1. Toss chicken with olive oil. Sprinkle with Italian salad dressing mix. Place in 5-quart **CROCK-POT**® slow cooker. Cover; cook on LOW 3 hours.

2. Coat large skillet with nonstick cooking spray. Add mushrooms and onion; cook 5 minutes over medium heat or until onions are tender, stirring occasionally.

3. Add soup, broccoli, cream cheese and sherry to skillet; cook until hot. Transfer to **CROCK-POT**® slow cooker. Cover; cook on LOW 1 hour. Serve chicken and sauce over pasta.

*Tip: For easier preparation, cut up the chicken and vegetables for this recipe the night before. Don't place the **CROCK-POT**® stoneware in the refrigerator. Instead, wrap the chicken and vegetables separately, and store in the refrigerator.*

Pork Loin with Sherry and Red Onions

Makes 8 servings

- 3 large red onions, thinly sliced
- 1 cup pearl onions, blanched and peeled
- 2 tablespoons unsalted butter or margarine
- 2½ pounds boneless pork loin, tied
- ½ teaspoon salt
- ½ teaspoon black pepper
- ½ cup cooking sherry
- 2 tablespoons Italian parsley, chopped
- 1½ tablespoons cornstarch
- 2 tablespoons water

1. Cook and stir red onions and pearl onions in butter in a medium skillet until tender.

2. Rub pork loin with salt and pepper and place in **CROCK-POT**® slow cooker. Add cooked onions, sherry and parsley. Cover; cook on LOW 8 to 10 hours or on HIGH 5 to 6 hours.

3. Remove pork loin from **CROCK-POT**® slow cooker; let stand 15 minutes before slicing. Meanwhile, combine cornstarch and water. Stir into cooking liquid and cook on LOW until sauce has thickened. Serve pork loin with onions and sherry sauce.

*Tip: For 5-, 6-, or 7-quart **CROCK-POT**® slow cookers, double all ingredients, except sherry, cornstarch and water.*

Pork and Tomato Ragout

Makes 6 servings

2	pounds pork stew meat, cut into 1-inch pieces
¼	cup all-purpose flour
3	tablespoons oil
1¼	cups white wine
2	pounds red potatoes, cut into ½-inch pieces
1	can (14½ ounces) diced tomatoes, undrained
1	cup finely chopped onion
1	cup water
½	cup finely chopped celery
2	cloves garlic, minced
½	teaspoon black pepper
1	cinnamon stick
3	tablespoons chopped fresh parsley

1. Toss pork with flour. Heat oil in large skillet over medium-high heat until hot. Add pork to skillet and brown on all sides. Transfer to **CROCK-POT®** slow cooker.

2. Add wine to skillet; bring to a boil, scraping up browned bits from bottom of skillet. Pour into **CROCK-POT®** slow cooker.

3. Add all remaining ingredients except parsley. Cover; cook on LOW 6 to 8 hours or until pork and potatoes are tender. Remove and discard cinnamon stick. Adjust seasonings, if desired. To serve, sprinkle with parsley.

*Tip: Vegetables such as potatoes and carrots can sometimes take longer to cook in a **CROCK-POT®** slow cooker than meat. Place evenly cut vegetables along the sides of the **CROCK-POT®** slow cooker when possible.*

Hearty Cassoulet

Makes 6 servings

  1   tablespoon olive oil
  1   large onion, finely chopped
  4   boneless skinless chicken thighs (about 1 pound), chopped
  ¼   pound smoked turkey sausage, finely chopped
  3   cloves garlic, minced
  1   teaspoon dried thyme
  ½   teaspoon black pepper
  4   tablespoons tomato paste
  2   tablespoons water
  3   cans (about 15 ounces each) Great Northern beans, rinsed and drained
  ½   cup dry bread crumbs
  3   tablespoons minced fresh parsley

1. Heat oil in large skillet over medium heat until hot. Add onion; cook and stir 5 minutes or until onion is tender. Stir in chicken, sausage, garlic, thyme and pepper. Cook 5 minutes or until chicken and sausage are browned.

2. Remove skillet from heat; stir in tomato paste and water until blended. Place beans and chicken mixture in **CROCK-POT®** slow cooker. Cover; cook on LOW 4 to 4½ hours.

3. Before serving, combine bread crumbs and parsley in small bowl. Sprinkle over top of cassoulet.

*Tip: When preparing ingredients for the **CROCK-POT®** slow cooker, cut into uniform pieces so that everything cooks evenly.*

Tarragon Turkey and Pasta

Makes 4 servings

1½ to 2 pounds turkey
    tenderloins
½ cup thinly sliced celery
¼ cup thinly sliced green
    onions
4 tablespoons fresh tarragon,
    minced, divided
¼ cup dry white wine
1 teaspoon salt
1 teaspoon black pepper
½ cup plain yogurt
1 tablespoon fresh minced
    Italian parsley
1 tablespoon lemon juice
1½ tablespoons cornstarch
2 tablespoons water
    Hot cooked pasta

1. Combine turkey, celery, green onions, 2 tablespoons fresh tarragon, wine, salt and pepper in **CROCK-POT®** slow cooker. Mix thoroughly. Cover; cook on LOW 6 to 8 hours or on HIGH 3½ to 4 hours, or until turkey is no longer pink.

2. Remove turkey and cut it into ½-inch-thick medallions. Turn **CROCK-POT®** slow cooker to HIGH. Add yogurt, remaining 2 tablespoons fresh tarragon, parsley and lemon juice to cooking liquid.

3. Combine cornstarch and water in small bowl. Stir mixture into cooking liquid. Cook until cooking liquid has thickened. Serve turkey medallions and tarragon sauce over pasta.

Tip: *For 5-, 6-, or 7-quart **CROCK-POT®** slow cookers, double all ingredients.*

Vegetarian Sausage Rice

Makes 8 cups

- 2 cups chopped green bell peppers
- 1 can (15 ounces) **dark kidney beans, drained and rinsed**
- 1 can (14½ ounces) **diced tomatoes with green bell peppers and onions, undrained**
- 1 cup **chopped onion**
- 1 cup **sliced celery**
- 1 cup **water, divided**
- ¾ cup **uncooked converted long-grain rice**
- 1¼ teaspoons **salt**
- 1 teaspoon **hot pepper sauce, plus additional for garnish**
- ½ teaspoon **dried thyme**
- ½ teaspoon **red pepper flakes**
- 3 **bay leaves**
- 1 package (8 ounces) **vegetable-protein breakfast patties, thawed**
- 2 tablespoons **extra-virgin olive oil**
- ½ cup **chopped fresh parsley**

1. Combine bell peppers, beans, tomatoes with juice, onion, celery, ½ cup water, rice, salt, hot sauce, thyme, pepper flakes and bay leaves in **CROCK-POT**® slow cooker. Cover; cook on LOW 4 to 5 hours. Remove and discard bay leaves.

2. Dice breakfast patties. Heat oil in large nonstick skillet over medium-high heat until hot. Add patties; cook 2 minutes or until lightly browned, scraping bottom of skillet occasionally.

3. Place patties in **CROCK-POT**® slow cooker. *Do not stir.* Add remaining ½ cup water to skillet; bring to a boil over high heat 1 minute, scraping up browned bits on bottom of skillet. Add liquid and parsley to slow cooker; stir gently to blend. Serve immediately with additional hot sauce, if desired.

Wild Rice and Mushroom Casserole

Makes 4 to 6 servings

2 tablespoons olive oil
½ medium red onion, finely diced
1 large green pepper, finely diced
8 ounces button mushrooms, thinly sliced
2 cloves garlic, minced
1 can (14 ounces) diced tomatoes, drained
1 teaspoon dried oregano
1 teaspoon paprika
2 tablespoons butter
2 tablespoons all-purpose flour
1½ cups milk
8 ounces pepper jack, Cheddar or Swiss cheese, shredded
1 teaspoon salt
½ teaspoon black pepper
2 cups wild rice, cooked according to package instructions

1. Coat **CROCK-POT**® slow cooker with nonstick cooking spray.

2. Heat oil in large skillet over medium heat until hot. Add onion, bell pepper and mushrooms. Cook and stir 5 to 6 minutes until vegetables soften. Add garlic, tomatoes, oregano and paprika. Continue to cook and stir until heated through. Transfer to large bowl to cool.

3. Melt butter in same skillet over medium heat; whisk in flour. Cook and stir until smooth and golden, about 4 to 5 minutes. Whisk in milk and bring to a boil. Whisk shredded cheese into boiling milk to produce rich, velvety sauce.

4. Combine cooked wild rice with vegetables in large bowl. Fold in cheese sauce to combine gently. Pour into prepared **CROCK-POT**® slow cooker. Cover; cook on LOW 4 to 6 hours or on HIGH 2 to 3 hours.

Turkey Tacos

Makes 8 servings

1   **pound lean ground turkey**
1   **medium onion, chopped**
1   **can (6 ounces) tomato paste**
½   **cup chunky salsa**
1   **tablespoon chopped fresh cilantro**
½   **teaspoon salt**
1   **tablespoon butter**
1   **tablespoon all-purpose flour**
¼   **teaspoon salt**
⅓   **cup milk**
½   **cup sour cream**
     Ground red pepper, to taste
8   **taco shells**

1. Brown turkey and onion in large skillet over medium heat, stirring to separate meat. Combine turkey mixture, tomato paste, salsa, cilantro and salt in **CROCK-POT**® slow cooker. Cover; cook on LOW 4 to 5 hours.

2. Just before serving, melt butter in small saucepan over low heat. Stir in flour and salt; cook 1 minute. Carefully stir in milk. Cook and stir over low heat until thickened. Remove from heat. Combine sour cream and sprinkle of ground red pepper in small bowl. Stir into hot milk mixture. Return to heat; cook over low heat 1 minute, stirring constantly.

3. To serve, spoon ¼ cup turkey mixture into each taco shell. Spoon sour cream mixture over taco filling.

Tip: *When adapting conventionally prepared recipes for your* **CROCK-POT**® *slow cooker, revise the amount of herbs and spices you use. For example, whole herbs and spices increase in flavor while ground spices tend to lose flavor during slow cooking. If you prefer, you can adjust the seasonings or add herbs and spices just before serving the dish.*

Big Al's Hot and Sweet Sausage Sandwich

Makes 8 to 10 servings

4 to 5 pounds hot Italian sausages
1 jar (26 ounces) spaghetti sauce
1 large onion, sliced (Vidalia preferred)
1 green bell pepper, cored, seeded and sliced
1 red bell pepper, cored, seeded and sliced
¼ cup packed dark brown sugar
Italian rolls, cut in half
Provolone cheese, sliced (optional)

1. Combine sausages, spaghetti sauce, onion, bell peppers and sugar in 5-quart **CROCK-POT®** slow cooker. Cover; cook on LOW 8 to 10 hours or on HIGH 4 to 6 hours.

2. Place sausages on rolls. Top with vegetable mixture. Add provolone cheese, if desired.

Tip: Browning the sausages before cooking them in the **CROCK-POT®** slow cooker isn't necessary but can help to enhance the flavor of the finished sandwich.

Three-Bean Mole Chili

Makes 4 to 6 servings

1   can (15½ ounces) chili beans in spicy sauce, undrained
1   can (15 ounces) pinto beans, rinsed and drained
1   can (15 ounces) black beans, rinsed and drained
1   can (14½ ounces) Mexican or chili-style diced tomatoes, undrained
1   large green bell pepper, diced
1   small onion, diced
½   cup beef, chicken or vegetable broth
¼   cup prepared mole paste*
2   teaspoons minced garlic
2   teaspoons ground cumin
2   teaspoons chili powder
2   teaspoons ground coriander (optional)
    Optional toppings: crushed tortilla chips, chopped cilantro, shredded cheese

Mole paste is available in the supermarket's Mexican section or in specialty markets.

Combine beans, tomatoes with juice, bell pepper, onion, broth, mole paste, garlic, cumin, chili powder and coriander, if desired, in **CROCK-POT**® slow cooker; mix well. Cover; cook on LOW 5 to 6 hours or until vegetables are tender. Serve with desired toppings.

Tip: Opening the lid and checking on food in the **CROCK-POT**® slow cooker can affect both cooking time and results. Due to the nature of slow cooking, there's no need to stir the food unless the recipe method says to do so.

Easy Parmesan Chicken

Makes 4 servings

8   ounces mushrooms, sliced

1   medium onion, cut into thin wedges

1   tablespoon olive oil

4   boneless skinless chicken breasts

1   jar (26 ounces) pasta sauce

½   teaspoon dried basil

¼   teaspoon dried oregano

1   bay leaf

½   cup (2 ounces) shredded part-skim mozzarella cheese

¼   cup grated Parmesan cheese
    Hot cooked spaghetti

1. Place mushrooms and onion in **CROCK-POT**® slow cooker.

2. Heat oil in large skillet over medium-high heat until hot. Lightly brown chicken on both sides. Place chicken in **CROCK-POT**® slow cooker. Pour pasta sauce over chicken; add basil, oregano and bay leaf. Cover; cook on LOW 6 to 7 hours or on HIGH 3 to 4 hours, or until chicken is tender. Remove and discard bay leaf.

3. Sprinkle chicken with cheeses. Cook, uncovered, on LOW 15 to 30 minutes or until cheeses have melted. Serve over spaghetti.

Tip: *Dairy products should be added at the end of the cooking time because they will curdle if cooked in the* **CROCK-POT**® *slow cooker for a long time.*

Simply Delicious Pork

Makes 6 servings

1½ **pounds boneless pork loin, cut into 6 pieces *or* 6 boneless pork loin chops**
4 **medium Golden Delicious apples, sliced**
3 **tablespoons packed light brown sugar**
1 **teaspoon ground cinnamon**
½ **teaspoon salt**

1. Place pork in **CROCK-POT**® slow cooker. Cover with apples.

2. Combine brown sugar, cinnamon and salt in small bowl; sprinkle over apples. Cover; cook on LOW 6 to 8 hours.

Simple Sides

Complement your main dish with a savory side

Corn on the Cob with Garlic Herb Butter

Makes 4 to 5 servings

½ cup (1 stick) unsalted butter, at room temperature
3 to 4 cloves garlic, minced
2 tablespoons finely minced fresh parsley
4 to 5 ears of corn, husked
Salt and black pepper, to taste

1. Thoroughly mix butter, garlic and parsley in small bowl.

2. Place each ear of corn on a piece of aluminum foil and generously spread butter on each ear. Season corn with salt and pepper and tightly seal foil.

3. Place corn in **CROCK-POT**® slow cooker; overlap ears if necessary. Add enough water to come ¼ of the way up each ear. Cover; cook on LOW 4 to 5 hours or on HIGH 2 to 2½ hours or until done.

*Tip: Consider using your **CROCK-POT**® slow cooker as an "extra" oven or burner during the grilling season. For example, the **CROCK-POT**® slow cooker can cook other dishes while you monitor steaks on the grill.*

Jim's Mexican-Style Spinach

Makes 6 servings

3 packages (10 ounces each) frozen chopped spinach
1 tablespoon canola oil
1 onion, chopped
1 clove garlic, minced
2 Anaheim chilies, roasted,* peeled and minced
3 fresh tomatillos, roasted,** husks removed and chopped
6 tablespoons fat-free sour cream (optional)

*To roast chilies, heat heavy frying pan over medium-high heat until drop of water sizzles. Cook chilies, turning occasionally with tongs, until blackened all over. (Or, hold directly over gas flame with long-handled fork.) Place chilies in brown paper bag for 2 to 5 minutes. Remove chilies from bag and scrape off charred skin. Cut off top with seed core. Cut lengthwise into halves and with a knife tip, scrape out veins and any remaining seeds.

**To roast fresh tomatillos, heat heavy frying pan over medium heat. Leaving papery husks on, roast tomatillos, turning often, until husks are brown and interior flesh is soft, about 10 minutes. When cool enough to handle, remove and discard husks.

1. Place frozen spinach in **CROCK-POT**® slow cooker.

2. Heat oil in large skillet over medium heat until hot. Cook and stir onion and garlic until onion is soft but not browned, about 5 minutes. Add chilies and tomatillos; cook 3 to 4 minutes longer. Add mixture to **CROCK-POT**® slow cooker.

3. Cover; cook on LOW 4 to 6 hours. Stir before serving. Serve with dollops of sour cream, if desired.

Red Cabbage and Apples

Makes 4 to 6 servings

- 1 small head red cabbage, cored and thinly sliced
- 3 medium apples, peeled and grated
- ¾ cup sugar
- ½ cup red wine vinegar
- 1 teaspoon ground cloves
- 1 cup crisp-cooked and crumbled bacon (optional)

  Fresh apple slices (optional)

Combine cabbage, apples, sugar, vinegar and cloves in **CROCK-POT®** slow cooker. Cover; cook on HIGH 6 hours, stirring after 3 hours. To serve, sprinkle with bacon and garnish with apple slices, if desired.

Slow-Roasted Potatoes

Makes 3 to 4 servings

- 16 small new potatoes
- 3 tablespoons butter, cut into small pieces
- 1 teaspoon paprika
- ½ teaspoon salt
- ¼ teaspoon garlic powder

  Black pepper, to taste

Combine all ingredients in **CROCK-POT®** slow cooker; mix well. Cover; cook on LOW 7 hours or on HIGH 4 hours. Remove potatoes with slotted spoon to serving dish; cover with foil to keep warm. Add 1 to 2 tablespoons water to cooking liquid and stir until well blended. Pour over potatoes.

Deluxe Potato Casserole

Makes 8 to 10 servings

- 1 can (10¾ ounces) condensed cream of chicken soup, undiluted
- 1 container (8 ounces) sour cream
- ¼ cup chopped onion
- ¼ cup plus 3 tablespoons melted butter, divided
- 1 teaspoon salt
- 2 pounds red potatoes, peeled and chopped
- 2 cups (8 ounces) shredded Cheddar cheese
- 1½ to 2 cups stuffing mix

1. Combine soup, sour cream, onion, ¼ cup butter and salt in small bowl.

2. Combine potatoes and cheese in **CROCK-POT**® slow cooker. Pour soup mixture over potato mixture; mix well. Sprinkle stuffing mix over potato mixture; drizzle with remaining 3 tablespoons butter. Cover; cook on LOW 8 to 10 hours or on HIGH 5 to 6 hours, or until potatoes are tender.

Creamy Curried Spinach

Makes 6 to 8 servings

- 3 packages (10 ounces each) frozen spinach, thawed
- 1 onion, chopped
- 4 teaspoons minced garlic
- 2 tablespoons curry powder
- 2 tablespoons butter, melted
- ¼ cup chicken broth
- ¼ cup heavy cream
- 1 teaspoon lemon juice

Combine spinach, onion, garlic, curry powder, butter and broth in **CROCK-POT**® slow cooker. Cover; cook on LOW 3 to 4 hours or on HIGH 2 hours, or until done. Stir in cream and lemon juice 30 minutes before end of cooking time.

Deluxe Potato Casserole

Swiss Cheese Scalloped Potatoes

Makes 5 to 6 servings

2 **pounds baking potatoes, peeled and thinly sliced, divided**
½ **cup finely chopped yellow onion, divided**
¼ **teaspoon salt, divided**
¼ **teaspoon ground nutmeg, divided**
2 **tablespoons butter, cut into small pieces, divided**
½ **cup milk**
2 **tablespoons all-purpose flour**
3 **ounces Swiss cheese slices, torn into small pieces**
¼ **cup finely chopped green onions (optional)**

1. Layer half the potatoes, ¼ cup onion, ⅛ teaspoon salt, ⅛ teaspoon nutmeg and 1 tablespoon butter in **CROCK-POT®** slow cooker. Repeat layers. Cover; cook on LOW 7 hours or on HIGH 4 hours.

2. Remove potatoes with slotted spoon to serving dish and cover with foil to keep warm.

3. Blend milk and flour in small bowl until smooth. Stir mixture into cooking liquid. Add cheese; stir to combine. Turn **CROCK-POT®** slow cooker to HIGH. Cover; cook until slightly thickened, about 10 minutes. Stir. Pour cheese mixture over potatoes and serve. Garnish with chopped green onions, if desired.

Tip: Don't add water to the **CROCK-POT®** slow cooker, unless a recipe specifically says so. Foods don't lose much moisture during slow cooking, so follow recipe guidelines.

Risotto-Style Peppered Rice

Makes 4 to 6 servings

- 1 cup uncooked converted long-grain rice
- 1 medium green bell pepper, chopped
- 1 medium red bell pepper, chopped
- 1 cup chopped onion
- ½ teaspoon ground turmeric
- ⅛ teaspoon ground red pepper (optional)
- 1 can (14½ ounces) fat-free chicken broth
- 4 ounces Monterey Jack cheese with jalapeño peppers, cubed
- ½ cup milk
- 4 tablespoons butter, cut into small pieces
- 1 teaspoon salt

1. Place rice, bell peppers, onion, turmeric and ground red pepper, if desired, in **CROCK-POT**® slow cooker. Stir in broth. Cover; cook on LOW 4 to 5 hours or until rice is tender and broth is absorbed.

2. Stir in cheese, milk, butter and salt; fluff rice with fork. Cover; cook on LOW 5 minutes or until cheese melts.

Tip: *Dairy products should be added at the end of the cooking time because they will curdle if cooked in the* **CROCK-POT**® *slow cooker for a long time.*

Herbed Fall Vegetables

Makes 6 servings

2   medium Yukon Gold potatoes, peeled and cut into ½-inch dice
2   medium sweet potatoes, peeled and cut into ½-inch dice
3   parsnips, peeled and cut into ½-inch dice
1   medium head fennel, sliced and cut into ½-inch dice
½   to ¾ cup chopped fresh herbs, such as tarragon, parsley, sage or thyme
4   tablespoons (½ stick) butter, cut into small pieces
1   cup chicken broth
1   tablespoon Dijon mustard
1   tablespoon salt
    Black pepper, to taste

1. Combine potatoes, parsnips, fennel, herbs and butter in **CROCK-POT**® slow cooker.

2. Whisk together broth, mustard, salt and pepper in small bowl. Pour mixture over vegetables. Cover; cook on LOW 4½ hours or on HIGH 3 hours, or until vegetables are tender, stirring occasionally to ensure even cooking.

*Tip: When adapting conventionally prepared recipes for your **CROCK-POT**® slow cooker, revise the amount of herbs and spices you use. For example, whole herbs and spices increase in flavor while ground spices tend to lose flavor during slow cooking. If you prefer, you can adjust the seasonings or add herbs and spices just before serving the dish.*

Spanish Paella-Style Rice

Makes 6 servings

- **2** cans (14½ ounces each) chicken broth
- **1½** cups uncooked converted long-grain rice
- **1** small red bell pepper, diced
- **⅓** cup dry white wine or water
- **½** teaspoon saffron threads, crushed *or* ½ teaspoon ground turmeric
- **⅛** teaspoon red pepper flakes
- **½** cup frozen peas, thawed Salt, to taste

1. Combine broth, rice, bell pepper, wine, saffron and pepper flakes in **CROCK-POT®** slow cooker; mix well. Cover; cook on LOW 4 hours or until liquid is absorbed.

2. Stir in peas. Cover; cook 15 to 30 minutes or until peas are hot. Season with salt.

Tip: Paella can contain a variety of meats as well. For more authenticity—and to turn this dish into a delicious main course—add ½ cup cooked ham, chicken, chorizo or seafood when you add the peas.

Rustic Cheddar Mashed Potatoes

Makes 8 servings

2 pounds russet potatoes, peeled and diced

1 cup water

⅓ cup butter, cut into small pieces

½ to ¾ cup milk

1¼ teaspoons salt

½ teaspoon black pepper

½ cup finely chopped green onions

½ to ¾ cup (2 to 3 ounces) shredded Cheddar cheese

1. Combine potatoes and water in **CROCK-POT®** slow cooker; dot with butter. Cover; cook on LOW 6 hours or on HIGH 3 hours, or until potatoes are tender. Transfer potatoes to large mixing bowl.

2. Using electric mixer at medium speed, whip potatoes until well blended. Add milk, salt and pepper; whip until well blended.

3. Stir in green onions and cheese; cover. Let stand 15 minutes to allow flavors to blend and cheese to melt.

Cheesy Broccoli Casserole

Makes 4 to 6 servings

2 packages (10 ounces each) chopped broccoli, thawed
1 can (10¾ ounces) condensed cream of celery soup, undiluted
1¼ cups shredded sharp Cheddar cheese, divided
¼ cup minced onions
½ teaspoon celery seed
1 teaspoon paprika
1 teaspoon hot pepper sauce
1 cup crushed potato chips or saltine crackers

1. Coat **CROCK-POT**® slow cooker with nonstick cooking spray. Combine broccoli, soup, 1 cup cheese, onions, celery seed, paprika and hot sauce in **CROCK-POT**® slow cooker; mix well. Cover; cook on LOW 5 to 6 hours or on HIGH 2½ to 3 hours, or until done.

2. Uncover; sprinkle top with potato chips and remaining ¼ cup cheese. Cook, uncovered, on LOW 30 to 60 minutes or on HIGH 15 to 30 minutes, or until cheese melts.

Tip: *For a change in taste, prepare with thawed chopped spinach instead of broccoli, and top with crushed crackers or spicy croutons to complement the cheesy crust.*

Orange-Spiced Sweet Potatoes

Makes 8 servings

 2 pounds sweet potatoes, peeled and diced
 ½ cup packed dark brown sugar
 ½ cup (1 stick) butter, cut into small pieces
 1 teaspoon ground cinnamon
 ½ teaspoon ground nutmeg
 ½ teaspoon grated orange peel
   Juice of 1 medium orange
 ¼ teaspoon salt
 1 teaspoon vanilla
   Chopped toasted pecans (optional)

Place all ingredients, except pecans, in **CROCK-POT**® slow cooker. Cover; cook on LOW 4 hours or on HIGH 2 hours or until potatoes are tender. Sprinkle with pecans before serving, if desired.

Tip: For a creamy variation, mash potatoes with a hand masher or electric mixer, and add ¼ cup milk or whipping cream for moist consistency. Sprinkle with cinnamon-sugar, and sprinkle on toasted pecans, if desired.

Wild Rice with Fruit and Nuts

Makes 6 to 8 servings

2 cups wild rice (or wild rice blend), rinsed*

½ cup dried cranberries

½ cup California sun-dried raisins, chopped

½ cup chopped dried apricots

½ cup almond slivers, toasted**

5 to 6 cups chicken broth

1 cup orange juice

2 tablespoons butter, melted

1 teaspoon cumin

2 green onions, thinly sliced

2 to 3 tablespoons chopped fresh parsley

Salt and black pepper, to taste

*Do not use parboiled rice or a blend containing parboiled rice.

**To toast almonds, spread in single layer on baking sheet. Bake in preheated 350°F oven 8 to 10 minutes or until golden brown, stirring frequently.

1. Combine wild rice, cranberries, raisins, apricots and almonds in **CROCK-POT**® slow cooker.

2. Combine 5 cups chicken broth, orange juice, butter and cumin in a medium bowl. Pour mixture over rice; mix well. Cover; cook on LOW 7 hours or on HIGH 2½ to 3 hours. Stir once, adding more hot broth if necessary.

3. When rice is soft to the bite, add green onions, parsley, salt and pepper. Cover; cook 10 minutes longer.

Asparagus and Cheese

Makes 4 to 6 servings

2 cups crushed saltine crackers

1 can (10¾ ounces) condensed cream of asparagus soup, undiluted

1 can (10¾ ounces) condensed cream of chicken soup, undiluted

⅔ cup slivered almonds

4 ounces American cheese, cut into cubes

1 egg

1½ pounds fresh asparagus, trimmed

Combine crackers, soups, almonds, cheese and egg in large bowl; stir well. Pour into **CROCK-POT®** slow cooker. Add asparagus, and stir to coat. Cover; cook on HIGH 3 to 3½ hours or until asparagus is tender. Garnish as desired.

*Tip: Cooking times are guidelines. **CROCK-POT®** slow cookers, just like ovens, cook differently depending on a variety of factors. For example, cooking times will be longer at higher altitudes. You may need to slightly adjust cooking times for your **CROCK-POT®** slow cooker.*

Pesto Rice and Beans

Makes 8 servings

- 1 can (15 ounces) Great Northern beans, rinsed and drained
- 1 can (14 ounces) chicken broth
- ¾ cup uncooked converted long-grain rice
- 1½ cups frozen cut green beans, thawed and drained
- ½ cup prepared pesto
  Grated Parmesan cheese (optional)

1. Combine beans, broth and rice in **CROCK-POT**® slow cooker. Cover; cook on LOW 2 hours.

2. Stir in green beans. Cover; cook 1 hour or until rice and beans are tender.

3. Turn off **CROCK-POT**® slow cooker and transfer stoneware to heatproof surface. Stir in pesto and Parmesan cheese, if desired. Let stand, covered, 5 minutes or until cheese is melted. Serve immediately.

*Tip: Choose converted long-grain rice (or Arborio rice when suggested) or wild rice for best results. Long, slow cooking can turn other types of rice into mush; if you prefer to use another type of rice instead of converted rice, cook it on the stove-top and add it to the **CROCK-POT**® slow cooker during the last 15 minutes of cooking.*

Winter
Warm-Ups
Cozy up to your seasonal favorites

Slow Cooker Cassoulet

Makes 4 servings

- 1 **pound white beans, such as Great Northern**
  Boiling water to cover beans
- 1 **tablespoon butter**
- 1 **tablespoon canola oil**
- 4 **veal shanks, 1½ inches thick, tied for cooking**
- 3 **cups beef broth**
- 4 **ounces maple-smoked bacon or pancetta, diced**
- 3 **cloves garlic, smashed**
- 1 **sprig each thyme and savory *or* a bouquet garni of 1 tablespoon each**
- 2 **whole cloves**
  Salt and pepper, to taste
- 4 **mild Italian sausages**

1. Rinse and sort beans and place in large bowl; cover completely with water. Soak 6 to 8 hours or overnight. (To quick-soak beans, place beans in large saucepan; cover with water. Bring to a boil over high heat. Boil 2 minutes. Remove from heat; let soak, covered, 1 hour.) Drain beans; discard water.

2. Heat butter and oil in large skillet over medium-high heat until hot. Sear shanks on all sides until browned. Transfer to **CROCK-POT**® slow cooker. Add broth, bacon, garlic, beans, herbs and cloves. Add enough water to cover beans, if needed. Cover; cook on LOW 8 hours. After 4 hours, check liquid and add boiling water as needed.

3. Before serving, season with salt and pepper. Grill sausages; serve with cassoulet.

Fresh Herbed Turkey Breast

Makes 8 servings

2   tablespoons butter, softened

¼   cup fresh sage, minced

¼   cup fresh tarragon, minced

1   clove garlic, minced

1   teaspoon black pepper

½   teaspoon salt

1   split turkey breast (about 4 pounds)

1½   tablespoons cornstarch

1. Thaw turkey breast, if frozen. Remove skin and discard. Combine butter, sage, tarragon, garlic, pepper and salt. Rub butter mixture all over turkey breast.

2. Place turkey breast in **CROCK-POT**® slow cooker. Cover; cook on LOW 8 to 10 hours or on HIGH 4 to 5 hours or until turkey is no longer pink in the center.

3. Transfer turkey breast to serving platter; cover with foil to keep warm. Turn **CROCK-POT**® slow cooker to HIGH; slowly whisk in cornstarch to thicken cooking liquid. When the sauce is thick and smooth, pour over turkey breast. Slice to serve.

*Tip: For 5-, 6-, or 7-quart **CROCK-POT**® slow cookers, double all ingredients.*

Harvest Bistro Pork Pot Roast

Makes 6 to 8 servings

- 2 large onions, peeled and quartered
- 3 stalks celery, cut into 1- to 2-inch pieces
- 1 cup fresh whole cranberries
- 1 large pear, cored and cut into 8 wedges
- 1 large red cooking apple, cored and cut into 8 wedges
- 1 quince, peeled and chopped (optional)
- 2 tablespoons fresh thyme *or* 2 teaspoons dried thyme
- ⅔ cup packed dark brown sugar
- 2 teaspoons salt, divided
- 3 pounds fresh lean pork butt roast, cut into 2- to 3-inch pieces
- 1 cup chicken broth
- 6 to 8 ounces Brie cheese, chopped

  Fresh thyme (optional)

1. Combine onions, celery, cranberries, pear, apple and quince, if desired, in **CROCK-POT®** slow cooker. Sprinkle with thyme, sugar and 1 teaspoon salt. Place pork on top of mixture. Pour broth over pork. Sprinkle with ½ teaspoon salt. Cover; cook on LOW 7 hours.

2. Sprinkle cheese over pork. Cover; cook on LOW 1 hour. Transfer pork to serving platter. Arrange vegetables and fruits around pork. Season with remaining salt, if desired. Garnish with thyme, if desired.

Autumn Chicken

Makes 10 to 12 servings

1	can (14 ounces) whole artichoke hearts, drained
1	can (14 ounces) whole mushrooms, divided
12	boneless skinless chicken breasts
1	jar (6½ ounces) marinated artichoke hearts, with liquid
¾	cup white wine
½	cup balsamic vinaigrette
	Hot cooked noodles
	Paprika for garnish (optional)

Spread whole artichokes over bottom of **CROCK-POT**® slow cooker. Top with half of mushrooms. Layer chicken over mushrooms. Add marinated artichoke hearts with liquid. Add remaining mushrooms. Pour in wine and vinaigrette. Cover; cook on LOW 4 to 5 hours. Serve over noodles. Garnish with paprika, if desired.

*Tip: Opening the lid and checking on food in the **CROCK-POT**® slow cooker can affect both cooking time and results. Due to the nature of slow cooking, there's no need to stir the food unless the recipe method says to do so.*

Harvest Ham Supper

Makes 6 servings

6	carrots, cut into 2-inch pieces
3	medium sweet potatoes, quartered
1	to 1½ pounds boneless ham
1	cup maple syrup

1. Arrange carrots and potatoes in bottom of **CROCK-POT**® slow cooker to form rack.

2. Place ham on top of vegetables. Pour syrup over ham and vegetables. Cover; cook on LOW 6 to 8 hours.

Autumn Chicken

Pork Roast Landaise

Makes 4 to 6 servings

2	tablespoons olive oil
2½	pounds boneless center-cut pork loin roast
	Salt and pepper, to taste
1	medium onion, diced
2	large cloves garlic, minced
2	teaspoons dried thyme
2	parsnips, cut into ¾-inch slices
¼	cup red wine vinegar
¼	cup sugar
½	cup port or sherry wine
2	cups chicken broth, divided
2	tablespoons cornstarch
3	pears, cored and sliced ¾ inch thick
1½	cups pitted prunes

1. Heat olive oil in large saucepan over medium-high heat. Season pork roast with salt and pepper; brown roast on all sides in saucepan. Place roast in **CROCK-POT**® slow cooker.

2. Add onion and garlic to saucepan. Cook and stir over medium heat 2 to 3 minutes. Stir in thyme. Transfer to **CROCK-POT**® slow cooker. Add parsnips; stir well.

3. Combine vinegar and sugar in same saucepan. Cook over medium heat, stirring constantly, until mixture thickens into syrup. Add port and cook 1 minute more. Add 1¾ cups chicken broth. Combine remaining ¼ cup of broth with cornstarch in small bowl. Whisk in cornstarch mixture, and cook until smooth and slightly thickened. Pour into **CROCK-POT**® slow cooker.

4. Cover; cook on LOW 8 hours or on HIGH 4 hours. Add pears and prunes during last 30 minutes of cooking.

Fall Beef and Beer Casserole

Makes 4 to 6 servings

- 2 tablespoons oil
- 1½ pounds beef for stew, cut into 1-inch cubes
- 2 tablespoons all-purpose flour
- 1 cup beef broth
- 2 cups brown ale or beer
- 1 cup water
- 1 onion, sliced
- 2 carrots, sliced
- 1 leek, sliced
- 2 stalks celery, sliced
- 1 cup mushrooms, sliced
- 1 turnip, cubed
- 1 teaspoon mixed herbs

1. Heat oil in large skillet over medium-high heat until hot. Cook beef until browned on all sides. Lower heat and add flour to skillet. Cook and stir 2 minutes. Gradually add broth, ale and water; bring to boil. Transfer mixture to **CROCK-POT®** slow cooker.

2. Add remaining ingredients. Cover; cook on low 8 to 10 hours or on HIGH 4 to 6 hours.

Tip: *To remove a small amount of fat from dishes cooked in the **CROCK-POT®** slow cooker, lightly pull a sheet of clean paper towel over the surface, letting the grease be absorbed by the paper towel. Repeat this process as necessary.*

Golden Harvest Pork Stew

Makes 4 servings

1 pound boneless pork cutlets, cut into 1-inch pieces
2 tablespoons all-purpose flour, divided
1 tablespoon vegetable oil
2 medium Yukon Gold potatoes, unpeeled and cut into 1-inch cubes
1 large sweet potato, peeled and cut into 1-inch cubes
1 cup chopped carrots
1 ear corn, broken into 4 pieces *or* ½ cup corn
½ cup chicken broth
1 jalapeño pepper,* seeded and finely chopped
1 clove garlic, minced
1 teaspoon salt
¼ teaspoon black pepper
¼ teaspoon dried thyme
   Chopped parsley

Jalapeño peppers can sting and irritate the skin, so wear rubber gloves when handling peppers and do not touch eyes.

1. Toss pork pieces with 1 tablespoon flour; set aside. Heat oil in large skillet over medium-high heat until hot. Add pork; cook until browned on all sides. Transfer to **CROCK-POT®** slow cooker.

2. Add remaining ingredients, except parsley and 1 tablespoon flour. Cover; cook on LOW 5 to 6 hours.

3. Combine remaining 1 tablespoon flour and ¼ cup cooking liquid from stew in small bowl; stir until smooth. Stir flour mixture into stew. Cook on HIGH 10 minutes or until thickened. To serve, sprinkle with parsley.

Shelby Slow Cooker Rouladen

Makes 6 to 8 servings

12	pieces top round beef, pounded thin (¼ inch thick)
	Salt and black pepper, to taste
	Garlic pepper, to taste
4	tablespoons Dijon mustard
1½	cups chopped onions
1½	cups chopped dill pickles
4	tablespoons (½ stick) butter
5	tablespoons all-purpose flour
2	cans (14½ ounces each) beef broth
16	ounces baby carrots
4	stalks celery, cut into 1-inch pieces

1. Season beef with salt, black pepper and garlic pepper. Spread each piece with 1 teaspoon mustard; top with 2 tablespoons each onion and pickles. Fold long edges over filling. Starting at short side, tightly roll up each beef piece. Secure with toothpick.

2. Coat large nonstick skillet with cooking spray. Heat over medium-high heat. Brown beef rolls in batches. Remove from skillet.

3. In same skillet, melt butter. Add flour. Cook and stir 1 minute. Add beef broth, stirring constantly. Cook and stir until mixture thickens.

4. Pour half of broth mixture into **CROCK-POT**® slow cooker. Add carrots and celery; top with beef rolls; pour in remaining broth mixture. Cover; cook on LOW 8 to 10 hours or on HIGH 4 to 5 hours until beef is tender.

Turkey with Pecan-Cherry Stuffing

Makes 8 servings

- **1** fresh or frozen boneless turkey breast (about 3 to 4 pounds)
- **2** cups cooked rice
- **⅓** cup chopped pecans
- **⅓** cup dried cherries *or* cranberries
- **1** teaspoon poultry seasoning
- **¼** cup peach, apricot or plum preserves
- **1** teaspoon Worcestershire sauce

1. Thaw turkey breast, if frozen. Remove skin and discard. Cut slices three-fourths of the way through turkey at 1-inch intervals.

2. Stir together rice, pecans, cherries and poultry seasoning in large bowl. Stuff rice mixture between slices. If necessary, skewer turkey lengthwise to hold it together.

3. Place turkey in **CROCK-POT**® slow cooker. Cover; cook on LOW 5 to 6 hours or until turkey registers 170°F on meat thermometer inserted into thickest part of breast, not touching stuffing.

4. Stir together preserves and Worcestershire sauce. Spoon over turkey. Cover; let stand for 5 minutes. Remove skewer before serving.

Tip: *Skinless cuts of poultry are best for the **CROCK-POT**® slow cooker because the skin can shrivel and curl during cooking.*

Barley Beef Stroganoff

Makes 4 servings

⅔ cup uncooked pearl barley (not quick-cooking)

2½ cups fat-free low-sodium vegetable broth or water

1 package (6 ounces) sliced mushrooms

½ teaspoon dried marjoram

½ pound 95% lean ground beef

½ cup chopped celery

½ cup minced green onion

½ teaspoon black pepper

¼ cup fat-free half-and-half

Minced fresh parsley (optional)

1. Place barley, broth, mushrooms and marjoram in **CROCK-POT®** slow cooker. Cover; cook on LOW 6 to 7 hours.

2. Cook and stir ground beef in large nonstick skillet over medium heat until browned and crumbly, about 7 minutes. Drain and discard fat. Add celery, green onion and pepper; cook and stir 3 minutes. Transfer to **CROCK-POT®** slow cooker.

3. Mix in half-and-half. Cover; cook on HIGH 10 to 15 minutes, until beef is hot and vegetables are tender. Garnish with parsley, if desired.

*Tip: Browning ground beef before adding it to the **CROCK-POT®** slow cooker helps reduce the fat. Just remember to drain off the fat in the skillet before transferring the meat to the **CROCK-POT®** slow cooker.*

Beef Stew with Bacon, Onion and Sweet Potatoes

Makes 4 servings

- 1 pound beef for stew, cut into 1-inch chunks
- 1 can (14½ ounces) beef broth
- 2 medium sweet potatoes, peeled and cut into 2-inch chunks
- 1 large onion, cut into 1½-inch chunks
- 2 slices thick-cut bacon, diced
- 1 teaspoon dried thyme
- 1 teaspoon salt
- ¼ teaspoon black pepper
- 2 tablespoons cornstarch
- 2 tablespoons water

1. Coat **CROCK-POT®** slow cooker with nonstick cooking spray. Combine all ingredients, except cornstarch and water, in **CROCK-POT®** slow cooker; mix well. Cover; cook on LOW 7 to 8 hours or on HIGH 4 to 5 hours, or until meat and vegetables are tender.

2. With slotted spoon, transfer beef and vegetables to serving bowl; cover with foil to keep warm.

3. Turn **CROCK-POT®** slow cooker to HIGH. Combine cornstarch and water; stir until smooth. Stir into cooking liquid. Cover; cook 15 minutes or until thickened. To serve, spoon sauce over beef and vegetables.

Heavenly Harvest Pork Roast

Makes 6 to 8 servings

- ¼ cup pomegranate juice
- ¼ cup sugar
- 1 tablespoon salt
- 1 tablespoon garlic salt
- 1 tablespoon steak seasoning
- 1 teaspoon black pepper
- 1 pork roast, any type (4 to 5 pounds)
- 2 pears, cored, peeled and sliced thick
- ½ orange with peel, sliced thick

1. Combine pomegranate juice and sugar in small saucepan. Cook over low heat, stirring until sugar dissolves, about 2 minutes. Pour into **CROCK-POT**® slow cooker.

2. Blend salt, garlic salt, steak seasoning and pepper in small mixing bowl. Rub mixture over roast. Place roast in **CROCK-POT**® slow cooker. Turn roast to cover with juice mixture.

3. Top roast with pear and orange slices. Cover; cook on HIGH 6 to 8 hours or until tender. Serve with juice and fruit slices.

*Tip: Unless you have a 5-, 6-, or 7-quart **CROCK-POT**® slow cooker, cut any roast larger than 2½ pounds in half so it cooks completely.*

Herbed Artichoke Chicken

Makes 6 servings

1½ **pounds skinless boneless chicken breasts**

1 **can (14 ounces) tomatoes, drained and diced**

1 **can (14 ounces) artichoke hearts in water, drained**

1 **small onion, chopped**

½ **cup kalamata olives, pitted and sliced**

1 **cup fat-free chicken broth**

¼ **cup dry white wine**

3 **tablespoons quick-cooking tapioca**

2 **teaspoons curry powder**

1 **tablespoon chopped fresh Italian parsley**

1 **teaspoon dried sweet basil**

1 **teaspoon dried thyme**

½ **teaspoon salt**

½ **teaspoon black pepper**

Combine all ingredients in **CROCK-POT**® slow cooker. Mix well. Cover; cook on LOW 6 to 8 hours or on HIGH 3½ to 4 hours, or until chicken is no longer pink in center.

Tip: For 5-, 6-, or 7-quart **CROCK-POT**® *slow cookers, double all ingredients, except chicken broth and white wine. Increase chicken broth and white wine by one-half.*

Slow-Simmered Curried Chicken

Makes 4 servings

1½   cups chopped onions
1   medium green bell pepper, chopped
1   pound boneless skinless chicken breasts or thighs, cut into bite-size pieces
1   cup medium salsa
2   teaspoons grated fresh ginger
½   teaspoon garlic powder
½   teaspoon red pepper flakes
¼   cup chopped fresh cilantro
1   teaspoon sugar
1   teaspoon curry powder
¾   teaspoon salt
    Hot cooked rice

1. Place onions and bell pepper in **CROCK-POT**® slow cooker. Place chicken on top.

2. Combine salsa, ginger, garlic powder and pepper flakes in small bowl; spoon over chicken. Cover; cook on LOW 5 to 6 hours or until chicken is tender.

3. Combine cilantro, sugar, curry powder and salt in small bowl; add to **CROCK-POT**® slow cooker and stir in. Cover; cook on HIGH 15 minutes or until hot. Serve over rice.

Turkey Breast with Barley-Cranberry Stuffing

Makes 6 servings

   2 cups reduced-sodium chicken broth
   1 cup uncooked quick-cooking barley
 ½ cup chopped onion
 ½ cup dried cranberries
   2 tablespoons slivered almonds, toasted*
 ½ teaspoon rubbed sage
 ½ teaspoon garlic-pepper seasoning
   1 fresh or thawed frozen bone-in turkey breast half (about 2 pounds), skinned
 ⅓ cup finely chopped fresh parsley

> *To toast almonds, spread in single layer on baking sheet. Bake in preheated 350°F oven 8 to 10 minutes or until golden brown, stirring frequently.

1. Thaw turkey breast, if frozen. Remove skin and discard.

2. Combine broth, barley, onion, cranberries, almonds, sage and garlic-pepper seasoning in **CROCK-POT**® slow cooker.

3. Coat large nonstick skillet with cooking spray. Heat over medium heat until hot. Brown turkey breast on all sides; add to **CROCK-POT**® slow cooker. Cover; cook on LOW 4 to 6 hours.

4. Transfer turkey to cutting board; cover with foil to keep warm. Let stand 10 to 15 minutes before carving. Stir parsley into sauce mixture in **CROCK-POT**® slow cooker. Serve over sliced turkey and stuffing.

*Tip: Browning poultry before cooking it in the **CROCK-POT**® slow cooker isn't necessary but helps to enhance the flavor and adds an oven-roasted appearance to the finished dish.*

Beef with Apples and Sweet Potatoes

Makes 6 servings

- 1 **boneless beef chuck shoulder roast (about 2 pounds)**
- 1 **can (40 ounces) sweet potatoes, drained**
- 2 **small onions, sliced**
- 2 **apples, cored and sliced**
- ½ **cup beef broth**
- 2 **cloves garlic, minced**
- 1 **teaspoon salt**
- 1 **teaspoon dried thyme, divided**
- ¾ **teaspoon black pepper, divided**
- 1 **tablespoon cornstarch**
- ¼ **teaspoon ground cinnamon**
- 2 **tablespoons cold water**

1. Trim excess fat from beef and discard. Cut beef into 2-inch pieces. Place beef, sweet potatoes, onions, apples, broth, garlic, salt, ½ teaspoon thyme and ½ teaspoon pepper in **CROCK-POT**® slow cooker. Cover; cook on LOW 8 to 9 hours.

2. Transfer beef, sweet potatoes and apples to platter; cover with foil to keep warm. Let cooking liquid stand 5 minutes to allow fat to rise. Skim off fat and discard.

3. Stir together cornstarch, remaining ½ teaspoon thyme, remaining ¼ teaspoon pepper, cinnamon and water until smooth; stir into cooking liquid. Cook 15 minutes on HIGH or until cooking liquid is thickened. Serve sauce over beef, sweet potatoes and apples.

Tip: Because **CROCK-POT**® slow cookers cook at a low heat for a long time, they're perfect for dishes calling for less-tender cuts of meat.

Spring & Summer
Sensations

Keep your kitchen cool during warm weather

Sweet and Sour Shrimp with Pineapple

Makes 4 servings

3   cans (8 ounces each) pineapple chunks, drained and 1 cup juice reserved
2   packages (6 ounces each) frozen snow peas, thawed
¼   cup cornstarch
⅓   cup sugar, plus 2 teaspoons
2   chicken bouillon cubes
2   cups boiling water
4   teaspoons soy sauce
1   teaspoon ground ginger
1   pound shrimp, peeled, deveined and cleaned
¼   cup cider vinegar
    Hot cooked rice

1. Drain pineapple chunks, reserving 1 cup juice. Place pineapple and snow peas in **CROCK-POT**® slow cooker.

2. Combine cornstarch and sugar in medium saucepan. Dissolve bouillon cubes in water and add to saucepan. Mix in 1 cup reserved pineapple juice, soy sauce and ginger. Bring to a boil and cook for 1 minute. Pour into **CROCK-POT**® slow cooker. Cover; cook on LOW 4½ to 5½ hours.

3. Add shrimp and vinegar. Cover; cook on LOW 30 minutes or until shrimp are done. Serve over hot rice.

Irish Stew

Makes 6 servings

1 cup fat-free reduced-sodium chicken broth

1 teaspoon dried marjoram

1 teaspoon dried parsley flakes

¾ teaspoon salt

½ teaspoon garlic powder

¼ teaspoon black pepper

1¼ pounds white potatoes, peeled and cut into 1-inch pieces

1 pound lean lamb for stew, cut into 1-inch cubes

8 ounces frozen cut green beans, thawed

2 small leeks, cut lengthwise into halves, then crosswise into slices

1½ cups coarsely chopped carrots

1. Combine broth, marjoram, parsley, salt, garlic powder and pepper in large bowl; mix well. Transfer to **CROCK-POT**® slow cooker.

2. Layer potatoes, lamb, green beans, leeks and carrots into **CROCK-POT**® slow cooker. Cover; cook on LOW 7 to 9 hours or until lamb is tender.

Tip: *If desired, thicken cooking liquid with a mixture of 1 tablespoon cornstarch and ¼ cup water. Stir mixture into cooking liquid; cook on HIGH 10 to 15 minutes or until thickened.*

Lemon Pork Chops

Makes 4 servings

1   tablespoon vegetable oil

4   boneless pork chops

3   cans (8 ounces each) tomato sauce

1   large onion, quartered and sliced (optional)

1   large green bell pepper, cut into strips

1   tablespoon lemon-pepper seasoning

1   tablespoon Worcestershire sauce

1   large lemon, quartered

    Lemon wedges (optional)

1. Heat oil in large skillet over medium-low heat until hot. Brown pork chops on both sides. Drain excess fat and discard. Transfer to **CROCK-POT**® slow cooker.

2. Combine tomato sauce, onion, if desired, bell pepper, lemon-pepper seasoning and Worcestershire. Add to **CROCK-POT**® slow cooker.

3. Squeeze juice from lemon quarters over mixture; drop squeezed peels into **CROCK-POT**® slow cooker. Cover; cook on LOW 6 to 8 hours or until pork is tender. Remove lemon wedges before serving. Garnish with additional lemon wedges, if desired.

*Tip: Browning pork before adding it to the **CROCK-POT**® slow cooker helps reduce the fat. Just remember to drain off the fat in the skillet before transferring the pork to the **CROCK-POT**® slow cooker.*

Stuffed Chicken Breasts

Makes 6 servings

6   boneless skinless chicken breasts
8   ounces feta cheese, crumbled
3   cups chopped fresh spinach leaves
⅓   cup oil-packed sun-dried tomatoes, drained and chopped
1   teaspoon minced lemon peel
1   teaspoon dried basil, oregano or mint
½   teaspoon garlic powder
    Black pepper, to taste
1   can (15 ounces) diced tomatoes, undrained
½   cup oil-cured olives*
    Hot cooked polenta

*If using pitted olives, add to slow cooker in final hour of cooking.

1. Place chicken breast between 2 pieces of plastic wrap. Using tenderizer mallet or back of skillet, pound breast until about ¼ inch thick. Repeat with remaining chicken.

2. Combine feta, spinach, sun-dried tomatoes, lemon peel, basil, garlic powder and pepper in medium bowl.

3. Lay pounded chicken, smooth side down, on work surface. Place approximately 2 tablespoons feta mixture on wide end of breast. Roll tightly. Repeat with remaining chicken.

4. Place rolled chicken, seam side down, in **CROCK-POT**® slow cooker. Top with diced tomatoes with juice and olives. Cover; cook on LOW 5½ to 6 hours or on HIGH 4 hours. Serve with polenta.

Greek-Style Chicken

Makes 4 to 6 servings

- 6 boneless skinless chicken thighs
- ½ teaspoon salt
- ½ teaspoon black pepper
- 1 tablespoon olive oil
- ½ cup chicken broth
- 1 lemon, thinly sliced
- ¼ cup pitted kalamata olives
- 1 clove garlic, minced
- ½ teaspoon dried oregano
  Hot cooked orzo or rice

1. Remove and discard visible fat from chicken. Season chicken with salt and pepper. Heat oil in large skillet over medium-high heat until hot. Brown chicken on all sides. Transfer to **CROCK-POT**® slow cooker.

2. Add broth, lemon, olives, garlic and oregano. Cover; cook on LOW 5 to 6 hours or until chicken is tender. Serve with orzo.

Tip: Freeze leftovers as individual portions; just reheat in a microwave for fast weeknight dinners!

Herbed Turkey Breast with Orange Sauce

Makes 4 to 6 servings

1	**large onion, chopped**
3	**cloves garlic, minced**
1	**teaspoon dried rosemary**
½	**teaspoon black pepper**
1	**boneless skinless turkey breast (2 to 3 pounds)**
1½	**cups orange juice**

1. Place onion in **CROCK-POT**® slow cooker. Combine garlic, rosemary and pepper in small bowl; set aside.

2. Cut slices about three-fourths of the way through turkey at 2-inch intervals. Rub garlic mixture between slices. Place turkey, cut side up, in **CROCK-POT**® slow cooker. Pour orange juice over turkey. Cover; cook on LOW 7 to 8 hours.

3. Serve sliced turkey with orange sauce.

Tip: *Don't peek! The* **CROCK-POT**® *slow cooker can take as long as 30 minutes to regain heat lost when the cover is removed. Only remove the cover when instructed to do so by the recipe.*

Best-Ever Barbecued Ribs

Makes 6 servings

- 1 **teaspoon paprika or smoked paprika**
- 1 **teaspoon salt**
- 1 **teaspoon dried thyme**
- ¼ **teaspoon black pepper**
- ⅛ **teaspoon ground red pepper**
- 3 **to 3½ pounds well-trimmed pork baby back ribs, cut into 4-rib pieces**
- ¼ **cup ketchup**
- 2 **tablespoons packed dark brown sugar**
- 1 **tablespoon Worcestershire sauce**
- 1 **tablespoon soy sauce**

1. Coat **CROCK-POT**® slow cooker with cooking spray. Combine paprika, salt, thyme, black pepper and red pepper; rub mixture onto meaty sides of ribs. Place ribs in **CROCK-POT**® slow cooker. Cover; cook on LOW 7 to 8 hours or on HIGH 3 to 3½ hours or until ribs are tender.

2. Combine ketchup, sugar, Worcestershire and soy sauce; mix well. Remove ribs from **CROCK-POT**® slow cooker; discard cooking liquid. Coat ribs with sauce; return to **CROCK-POT**® slow cooker and cook on HIGH 30 minutes, or until ribs are glazed.

*Tip: Spinning the cover until the condensation falls off will allow you to see inside the **CROCK-POT**® slow cooker without removing the lid; taking off the cover extends the cooking time.*

Caribbean Shrimp with Rice

Makes 4 servings

1	package (12 ounces) frozen shrimp, thawed
½	cup fat-free reduced-sodium chicken broth
1	clove garlic, minced
1	teaspoon chili powder
½	teaspoon salt
½	teaspoon dried oregano
1	cup frozen peas, thawed
½	cup diced tomatoes
2	cups cooked long-grain white rice

1. Combine shrimp, broth, garlic, chili powder, salt and oregano in **CROCK-POT®** slow cooker. Cover; cook on LOW 2 hours.

2. Add peas and tomatoes. Cover; cook on LOW 5 minutes. Stir in rice. Cover; cook on LOW 5 minutes longer, or until rice is heated through.

Corned Beef and Cabbage

Makes 6 servings

1	head cabbage (about 1½ pounds), cut into 6 wedges
4	ounces baby carrots
1	corned beef (about 3 pounds) with seasoning packet (perforate packet with knife tip)
4	cups water
⅓	cup prepared mustard
⅓	cup honey

1. Place cabbage and carrots in **CROCK-POT®** slow cooker. Place seasoning packet on top. Add corned beef, fat side up. Pour in water. Cover; cook on LOW 10 hours.

2. Remove and discard seasoning packet. Combine mustard and honey in small bowl. Slice beef; serve with vegetables and mustard sauce.

Saucy Tropical Turkey

Makes 6 servings

3 to 4 turkey thighs, skin removed (about 2½ pounds)
2 tablespoons vegetable oil
1 small onion, sliced
1 can (20 ounces) pineapple chunks, drained
1 red bell pepper, cubed
⅔ cup apricot preserves
3 tablespoons soy sauce
1 teaspoon grated lemon peel
1 teaspoon ground ginger
¼ cup cold water
2 tablespoons cornstarch
Hot cooked rice

1. Rinse turkey and pat dry. Heat oil in large skillet over medium-high heat until hot. Brown turkey on all sides. Place onion in **CROCK-POT**® slow cooker. Transfer turkey to **CROCK-POT**® slow cooker; top with pineapple and bell pepper.

2. Combine preserves, soy sauce, lemon peel and ginger in small bowl; mix well. Spoon over turkey. Cover; cook on LOW 6 to 7 hours.

3. Transfer turkey to serving platter; cover with foil to keep warm. Blend water and cornstarch until smooth; stir into cooking liquid. Cook, uncovered, on HIGH 15 minutes or until sauce is slightly thickened. Adjust seasonings, if necessary. Return turkey to **CROCK-POT**® slow cooker; cook until hot. Serve with rice.

Tip: *Recipes often provide a range of cooking times to account for variables, such as the temperature of the ingredients before cooking, the quantity of food in your* ***CROCK-POT****® slow cooker and the altitude; cooking times will be longer at higher altitudes.*

Jamaica-Me-Crazzy Chicken Tropicale

Makes 4 servings

2   medium sweet potatoes, peeled and cut into 2-inch pieces
1   can (8 ounces) water chestnuts, drained and sliced
1   cup golden raisins
1   can (20 ounces) pineapple tidbits in pineapple juice, drained and juice reserved
4   boneless skinless chicken breasts
4   teaspoons Jamaican jerk seasoning, or to taste
¼   cup dried onion flakes
3   tablespoons grated fresh ginger
2   tablespoons Worcestershire sauce
1   tablespoon grated lime peel
1   teaspoon cumin seed, slightly crushed
    Hot cooked rice (optional)

1. Place sweet potatoes in **CROCK-POT**® slow cooker. Add water chestnuts, raisins and pineapple tidbits; mix well.

2. Sprinkle chicken with jerk seasoning. Place chicken over potato mixture.

3. Combine reserved pineapple juice, onion flakes, ginger, Worcestershire, lime peel and cumin in small bowl. Pour mixture over chicken. Cover; cook on LOW 7 to 9 hours or on HIGH 3 to 4 hours, or until chicken and potatoes are fork-tender. Serve with rice, if desired.

Tip: *The flavor and aroma of crushed or ground herbs and spices may lessen during a longer cooking time. So, after slow cooking in your* **CROCK-POT**® *slow cooker, be sure to taste and adjust your seasonings before serving.*

Mu Shu Turkey

Makes 6 servings

- 1 can (16 ounces) plums, drained and pitted
- ½ cup orange juice
- ¼ cup finely chopped onion
- 1 tablespoon minced fresh ginger
- ¼ teaspoon ground cinnamon
- 1 pound boneless turkey breast, cut into thin strips
- 6 (7-inch) flour tortillas
- 3 cups coleslaw mix

1. Place plums in blender or food processor. Cover; blend until almost smooth. Combine plums, orange juice, onion, ginger and cinnamon in **CROCK-POT**® slow cooker; mix well.

2. Place turkey over plum mixture. Cover; cook on LOW 3 to 4 hours.

3. Remove turkey from **CROCK-POT**® slow cooker. Divide evenly among tortillas. Spoon about 2 tablespoons plum sauce over turkey in each tortilla; top with about ½ cup coleslaw mix. Fold up bottom edge of tortilla over filling, fold in sides and roll up to enclose filling. Repeat with remaining tortillas. Use remaining plum sauce for dipping.

Tip: *To slightly thicken a sauce in the* **CROCK-POT**® *slow cooker, remove the solid foods and leave the sauce in the* **CROCK-POT**® *slow cooker. Mix 1 to 2 tablespoons cornstarch with ¼ cup cold water until smooth. Stir mixture into the sauce and cook on HIGH until the sauce is thickened.*

Chutney Curried Chicken with Yogurt Sauce

Makes 4 servings

- 1 container (6 to 8 ounces) plain low-fat yogurt
- 2 teaspoons curry powder
- 1 teaspoon garlic salt
- ⅛ teaspoon ground red pepper
- 4 bone-in chicken breast halves, skin removed (2 to 2¼ pounds)
- 1 small onion, sliced
- ⅓ cup mango chutney (chop large pieces of mango, if necessary)
- 1 tablespoon lime juice
- 2 cloves garlic, minced
- 2 tablespoons cornstarch
- 2 tablespoons water
- 3 cups hot cooked linguini or lo mein noodles

  Optional toppings: Chopped cilantro, chopped peanuts, toasted coconut

1. Place yogurt in paper-towel-lined strainer over a bowl. Drain in refrigerator until serving time.

2. Combine curry powder, garlic salt and red pepper; sprinkle over chicken. Place onion in **CROCK-POT®** slow cooker; top with chicken. Combine chutney, lime juice and garlic; spoon over chicken. Cover; cook on LOW 5 to 6 hours or on HIGH 2½ to 3 hours or until chicken is tender.

3. With slotted spoon, transfer chicken to serving platter; cover with foil to keep warm. Turn **CROCK-POT®** slow cooker to HIGH. Combine cornstarch with water until smooth. Stir into cooking liquid. Cover; cook 15 minutes or until thickened. Spoon sauce over chicken; serve over linguini. Top with thickened yogurt, and garnish as desired.

Hungarian Lamb Goulash

Makes 6 servings

1	package (16 ounces) frozen cut green beans, thawed
1	cup chopped onion
1¼	pounds lean lamb for stew, cut into 1-inch cubes
1	can (15 ounces) chunky tomato sauce
1¾	cups fat-free reduced-sodium chicken broth
1	can (6 ounces) tomato paste
4	teaspoons paprika
	Hot cooked egg noodles

1. Place green beans and onion in **CROCK-POT**® slow cooker. Top with lamb.

2. Combine tomato sauce, broth, tomato paste and paprika in large bowl; mix well. Pour over lamb mixture. Cover; cook on LOW 6 to 8 hours. Stir goulash before serving over noodles.

BBQ Roast Beef

Makes 10 to 12 sandwiches

2	pounds boneless cooked roast beef
1	bottle (12 ounces) barbecue sauce
1½	cups water
10	to 12 sandwich rolls, halved

1. Combine roast beef, barbecue sauce and water in **CROCK-POT**® slow cooker. Cover; cook on LOW 2 hours.

2. Remove beef from **CROCK-POT**® slow cooker. Shred with 2 forks. Return beef to sauce; mix well. Serve on rolls.

Tip: Freeze leftovers as individual portions; just reheat in a microwave for fast meals!

Hungarian Lamb Goulash

Easy-Bake

Cakes & Breads

Moist and tender baked foods from your slow cooker

Orange Cranberry-Nut Bread

Makes 8 to 10 servings

2 cups all-purpose flour	2 teaspoons dried orange peel
1 teaspoon baking powder	⅔ cup boiling water
½ teaspoon baking soda	¾ cup sugar
¼ teaspoon salt	2 tablespoons shortening
½ cup chopped pecans	1 egg, lightly beaten
1 cup dried cranberries	1 teaspoon vanilla

1. Coat **CROCK-POT**® slow cooker with nonstick cooking spray. Blend flour, baking powder, baking soda and salt in medium bowl. Mix in pecans; set aside.

2. Combine cranberries and orange peel in separate medium bowl; pour boiling water over fruit mixture and stir. Add sugar, shortening, egg and vanilla; stir just until blended. Add flour mixture; stir just until blended.

3. Pour batter into **CROCK-POT**® slow cooker. Cover; cook on HIGH 1¼ to 1½ hours, or until edges begin to brown and cake tester inserted into center comes out clean. Remove stoneware from **CROCK-POT**® slow cooker. Cool on wire rack about 10 minutes; remove bread from stoneware and cool completely on rack.

*Tip: This recipe works best in round **CROCK-POT**® slow cookers.*

Baked Fudge Pudding Cake

Makes 6 to 8 servings

- **6 tablespoons unsweetened cocoa powder**
- **¼ cup all-purpose flour**
- **⅛ teaspoon salt**
- **4 eggs**
- **1⅓ cups sugar**
- **1 cup (2 sticks) unsalted butter, melted**
- **1 teaspoon vanilla**
- **Grated peel of 1 orange**
- **½ cup whipping cream**
- **Chopped toasted pecans**
- **Whipped cream or vanilla ice cream**

1. Coat **CROCK-POT®** slow cooker with nonstick cooking spray. Preheat **CROCK-POT®** slow cooker on LOW. Blend cocoa, flour and salt in small bowl; set aside.

2. Beat eggs in large bowl with electric mixer on medium-high speed until thickened. Gradually add sugar, beating about 5 minutes or until very thick and pale yellow. Mix in butter, vanilla and peel. Stir cocoa mixture into egg mixture. Add cream; mix until blended. Pour batter into **CROCK-POT®** slow cooker.

3. Cover opening of **CROCK-POT®** slow cooker with paper towel to collect condensation, making sure it doesn't touch pudding mixture. Place lid over paper towel. Cook on LOW 3 to 4 hours (do not cook on HIGH).

4. To serve, spoon into dishes. Sprinkle with toasted pecans, and top with whipped cream. Refrigerate leftovers.

Tip: Refrigerate leftover pudding cake in a covered container. To serve, reheat individual servings in the microwave for about 15 seconds. Or, make fudge truffles. Roll leftover cake into small balls and dip them into melted chocolate. Let stand until chocolate hardens.

Skinny Cornbread

Makes 8 servings

1¼ **cups all-purpose flour**
¾ **cup yellow cornmeal**
¼ **cup sugar**
1 **teaspoon baking powder**
1 **teaspoon baking soda**
1 **teaspoon seasoned salt**
1 **cup fat-free buttermilk**
¼ **cup cholesterol-free egg substitute**
¼ **cup canola oil**

1. Coat **CROCK-POT**® slow cooker with nonstick cooking spray.

2. Sift together flour, cornmeal, sugar, baking powder, baking soda and seasoned salt in large bowl. Make well in center of dry mixture. Pour in buttermilk, egg substitute and oil. Mix in dry ingredients just until moistened. Pour mixture into **CROCK-POT**® slow cooker.

3. Cook, covered, with lid slightly ajar to allow excess moisture to escape, on LOW 3 to 4 hours or on HIGH 45 minutes to 1½ hours, or until edges are golden and knife inserted into center comes out clean. Remove stoneware from **CROCK-POT**® slow cooker. Cool on wire rack about 10 minutes; remove bread from stoneware and cool completely on rack.

Tip: *This recipe works best in round **CROCK-POT**® slow cookers.*

Easy Chocolate Pudding Cake

Makes 16 servings

1 package (6-serving size) instant chocolate pudding and pie filling mix
3 cups milk
1 package (about 18 ounces) chocolate fudge cake mix, plus ingredients
   to prepare mix
   Crushed peppermint candies (optional)
   Whipped topping or ice cream (optional)

1. Coat 4-quart **CROCK-POT**® slow cooker with nonstick cooking spray. Place pudding mix in **CROCK-POT**® slow cooker. Whisk in milk.

2. Prepare cake mix according to package directions. Carefully pour cake mix into **CROCK-POT**® slow cooker. *Do not stir.* Cover; cook on HIGH 1½ hours or until cake tester inserted into center comes out clean.

3. Spoon into cup or onto plate; serve warm with crushed peppermint candies and whipped topping, if desired.

*Tip: Allow breads, cakes and puddings to cool at least 5 minutes before scooping or removing them from the **CROCK-POT®** stoneware.*

Spinach Gorgonzola Corn Bread

Makes 10 to 12 servings

2   boxes (8½ ounces each)
    cornbread mix

3   eggs

½   cup cream

1   box (10 ounces) frozen
    chopped spinach, thawed
    and drained

1   cup gorgonzola crumbles

1   teaspoon black pepper
    Paprika (optional)

1. Coat **CROCK-POT®** slow cooker with nonstick cooking spray.

2. Mix all ingredients in medium bowl. Place batter in **CROCK-POT®** slow cooker. Cover; cook on HIGH 1½ hours. Sprinkle top with paprika for more colorful crust, if desired. Let bread cool completely before inverting onto serving platter.

Tip: Cook only on HIGH setting for proper crust and texture.

Steamed Pumpkin Cake

Makes 12 servings

1½ cups all-purpose flour
1½ teaspoons baking powder
1½ teaspoons baking soda
1 teaspoon ground cinnamon
½ teaspoon salt
¼ teaspoon ground cloves
½ cup (1 stick) unsalted butter
2 cups packed light brown sugar
3 eggs, beaten
1 can (15 ounces) solid-pack pumpkin
Whipped cream (optional)

1. Make foil handles using three 18×2-inch strips of heavy-duty foil, or use regular foil folded to double thickness. Place in **CROCK-POT**® slow cooker; crisscross foil to form spoke design across bottom and up sides. Prepare 2½-quart casserole or soufflé dish that will fit in **CROCK-POT**® slow cooker stoneware by coating with nonstick cooking spray; set aside.

2. Combine flour, baking powder, baking soda, cinnamon, salt and cloves in medium bowl; set aside.

3. Beat butter, brown sugar and eggs in large bowl with electric mixer on medium speed until creamy. Beat in pumpkin. Stir in flour mixture. Spoon batter into prepared casserole.

4. Fill **CROCK-POT**® slow cooker with 1 inch of hot water. Place casserole into **CROCK-POT**® slow cooker. Cover; cook on HIGH 3 to 3½ hours or until wooden toothpick inserted into center comes out clean.

5. Use foil handles to lift casserole from **CROCK-POT**® slow cooker. Cool on wire rack 15 minutes. Invert onto serving platter. Cut into wedges; serve with whipped cream, if desired.

Banana Nut Bread

Makes 6 servings

1¾ cups all-purpose flour
 2 teaspoons baking powder
 ½ teaspoon salt
 ¼ teaspoon baking soda
 ⅓ cup butter or margarine
 ⅔ cup sugar
 2 eggs, well beaten
 2 tablespoons dark corn syrup
 3 ripe bananas, well mashed
 ½ cup chopped walnuts

1. Grease and flour **CROCK-POT**® slow cooker. Sift together flour, baking powder, salt and baking soda in small bowl; set aside

2. Cream butter in large bowl with electric mixer at medium-high speed until fluffy. Slowly add sugar, eggs, corn syrup and mashed bananas. Beat until smooth. Gradually add flour mixture to creamed mixture. Add walnuts and mix well. Pour into **CROCK-POT**® slow cooker. Cover; cook on HIGH 1¼ to 1½ hours or until toothpick inserted into center comes out clean.

3. Let cool, then invert bread onto serving platter.

Tip: *Allow breads, cakes and puddings to cool at least 5 minutes before scooping or removing them from the* **CROCK-POT**® *stoneware.*

Honey Whole-Grain Bread

Makes 8 to 10 servings

3 cups whole-wheat bread flour, divided

2 cups warm (not hot) whole milk

¾ to 1 cup all-purpose flour, divided

¼ cup honey

2 tablespoons vegetable oil

1 package active dry yeast

¾ teaspoon salt

1. Make foil handles using three 18×2-inch strips of heavy-duty foil, or use regular foil folded to double thickness. Place in **CROCK-POT**® slow cooker stoneware; crisscross foil to form spoke design across bottom and up sides. Prepare 1-quart casserole, soufflé dish or other high-sided baking pan that will fit in **CROCK-POT**® slow cooker by coating with nonstick cooking spray; set aside.

2. Combine 1½ cups whole wheat flour, milk, ½ cup all-purpose flour, honey, oil, yeast and salt in large bowl. Beat with electric mixer at medium speed 2 minutes. Add remaining 1½ cups whole wheat flour and ¼ cup to ½ cup all-purpose flour until dough is no longer sticky. (If mixer has difficulty mixing dough, mix in remaining flours with wooden spoon.) Transfer to prepared casserole.

3. Place casserole in **CROCK-POT**® slow cooker. Cover; cook on HIGH 3 hours or until edges are browned.

4. Use foil handles to lift dish from **CROCK-POT**® slow cooker. Let stand 5 minutes. Unmold on wire rack to cool.

Peach-Pecan Upside-Down Cake

Makes 10 servings

- 1 can (8½ ounces) peach slices
- ⅓ cup packed light brown sugar
- 2 tablespoons butter or margarine, melted
- ¼ cup chopped pecans
- 1 package (16 ounces) pound cake mix, plus ingredients to prepare mix
- ½ teaspoon almond extract
  Whipped cream (optional)

1. Remove stoneware from 4-quart **CROCK-POT**® slow cooker. Make foil handles using three 18×2-inch strips of heavy-duty foil, or use regular foil folded to double thickness. Place in **CROCK-POT**® slow cooker; crisscross foil to form spoke design across bottom and up sides. Prepare 2-quart casserole or soufflé dish that will fit in **CROCK-POT**® slow cooker by coating with nonstick cooking spray; set aside.

2. Drain peach slices, reserving 1 tablespoon of juice. Combine reserved peach juice, brown sugar and butter in prepared casserole. Arrange peach slices on top of brown sugar mixture. Sprinkle with pecans.

3. Prepare cake mix according to package directions; stir in almond extract. Spread over peach mixture. Cover casserole with greased foil. Place pan into **CROCK-POT**® slow cooker (not into stoneware). Cover; cook on HIGH 1¼ to 1½ hours or until toothpick inserted into center comes out clean.

4. Use foil handles to remove casserole from **CROCK-POT**® slow cooker. Cool, uncovered, on wire rack for 10 minutes. Run narrow spatula around sides of casserole; invert onto serving plate. Serve warm with whipped cream, if desired.

Peanut Fudge Pudding Cake

Makes 4 servings

- 1 cup all-purpose flour
- 1 cup sugar, divided
- 1½ teaspoons baking powder
- ⅔ cup milk
- 2 tablespoons vegetable oil
- 1 teaspoon vanilla
- ½ cup peanut butter
- ¼ cup unsweetened cocoa powder
- 1 cup boiling water
- Chopped peanuts (optional)
- Vanilla ice cream (optional)

1. Coat **CROCK-POT®** slow cooker with nonstick cooking spray or butter. Combine flour, ½ cup sugar and baking powder in medium bowl. Add milk, oil, vanilla and peanut butter. Mix until well-blended. Pour batter into **CROCK-POT®** slow cooker.

2. Combine remaining ½ cup sugar and cocoa powder in small bowl. Stir in water. Pour into **CROCK-POT®** slow cooker. *Do not stir.*

3. Cover; cook on HIGH 1¼ to 1½ hours or until toothpick inserted into center comes out clean. Allow cake to rest 10 minutes, then scoop into serving dishes or invert onto serving platter. Serve warm with chopped peanuts and ice cream, if desired.

*Tip: Because this recipe makes its own fudge topping, be sure to spoon some of it from the bottom of the **CROCK-POT®** slow cooker when serving, or invert the cake for a luscious chocolatey finish.*

Hot Fudge Cake

Makes 6 to 8 servings

1¾ cups packed light brown sugar, divided
2 cups all-purpose flour
¼ cup plus 3 tablespoons unsweetened cocoa powder, divided, plus additional for dusting, if desired
2 teaspoons baking powder
1 teaspoon salt
1 cup milk
4 tablespoons (½ stick) butter, melted
1 teaspoon vanilla
3½ cups boiling water

1. Coat **CROCK-POT**® slow cooker with nonstick cooking spray or butter. Mix 1 cup sugar, flour, 3 tablespoons cocoa powder, baking powder and salt in medium bowl. Stir in milk, butter and vanilla. Mix until well-blended. Pour into **CROCK-POT**® slow cooker.

2. Blend remaining ¾ cup sugar and ¼ cup cocoa powder in small bowl. Sprinkle evenly over mixture in **CROCK-POT**® slow cooker. Pour in boiling water. *Do not stir.*

3. Cover; cook on HIGH 1¼ to 1½ hours or until toothpick inserted into center comes out clean. Allow cake to rest 10 minutes, then invert onto serving platter or scoop into serving dishes. Serve warm; dust with cocoa powder, if desired.

Spinach Spoon Bread

Makes 8 servings

- 1 package (10 ounces) frozen chopped spinach, thawed and squeezed dry
- 1 red bell pepper, diced
- 4 eggs, lightly beaten
- 1 cup cottage cheese
- 1 package (5½ ounces) cornbread mix
- 6 green onions, sliced
- ½ cup (1 stick) butter, melted
- 1¼ teaspoons seasoned salt

1. Coat **CROCK-POT®** slow cooker with nonstick cooking spray. Preheat on HIGH.

2. Combine all ingredients in large bowl; mix well. Pour batter into prepared **CROCK-POT®** slow cooker. Cook, covered, with lid slightly ajar to allow excess moisture to escape, on LOW 3 to 4 hours or on HIGH 1¾ to 2 hours, or until edges are golden and knife inserted in center of bread comes out clean.

3. Loosen edges and bottom with knife and invert onto plate. Cut into wedges to serve. Or, serve bread spooned from **CROCK-POT®** slow cooker.

Chocolate Chip Lemon Loaf

Makes 8 servings

¾ **cup granulated sugar**

½ **cup shortening**

2 **eggs, lightly beaten**

1⅔ **cups all-purpose flour**

1½ **teaspoons baking powder**

¼ **teaspoon salt**

¾ **cup milk**

½ **cup chocolate chips**

Grated peel of 1 lemon

Juice of 1 lemon

¼ **to** ½ **cup powdered sugar**

Melted chocolate (optional)

1. Make foil handles using three 18×2-inch strips of heavy-duty foil, or use regular foil folded to double thickness. Place in **CROCK-POT**® slow cooker; crisscross foil to form spoke design across bottom and up sides. Preheat **CROCK-POT**® slow cooker on LOW. Prepare 2-quart casserole or soufflé dish that will fit in **CROCK-POT**® slow cooker stoneware (or 2-pound coffee can) by coating with nonstick cooking spray.

2. Sift together flour, baking powder and salt in medium bowl; set aside.

3. Beat granulated sugar and shortening in large bowl with electric mixer at medium-high speed until blended. Add eggs, one at a time, mixing well after each addition. Add flour mixture and milk alternately. Stir in chocolate chips and lemon peel.

4. Spoon batter into prepared casserole. Cover with greased foil. Place dish in preheated **CROCK-POT**® slow cooker. Cook, covered, with lid slightly ajar to allow excess moisture to escape, on LOW 3 to 4 hours or on HIGH 1¾ to 2 hours, or until edges are golden and knife inserted into center of loaf comes out clean. Remove dish from **CROCK-POT**® slow cooker; remove foil. Place loaf on wire rack to cool completely.

5. Combine lemon juice and ¼ cup powdered sugar in small bowl until smooth. Add more sugar as needed to reach desired glaze consistency. Pour glaze over loaf. Drizzle loaf with melted chocolate, if desired.

How
Sweet
It Is

Save room for dessert!

Bananas Foster

Makes 12 servings

12	bananas, cut into quarters
1	cup flaked coconut
1	teaspoon ground cinnamon
½	teaspoon salt
1	cup dark corn syrup
⅔	cup butter, melted
2	teaspoons grated lemon peel
¼	cup lemon juice
2	teaspoons rum
12	slices pound cake
1	quart vanilla ice cream

1. Combine bananas and coconut in **CROCK-POT**® slow cooker. Stir together cinnamon, salt, corn syrup, butter, lemon peel, lemon juice and rum in medium bowl. Pour over bananas.

2. Cover; cook on LOW 1 to 2 hours. Arrange bananas on pound cake slices. Top with ice cream and pour on warm sauce.

*Tip: Consider using your **CROCK-POT**® slow cooker as an "extra" oven or burner when entertaining. For example, the **CROCK-POT**® slow cooker can cook and keep warm a show-stopping dessert while the holiday roast is in the oven.*

"Peachy Keen" Dessert Treat

Makes 8 to 12 servings

1⅓ cups uncooked
old-fashioned oats
1 cup granulated sugar
1 cup packed light brown sugar
⅔ cup buttermilk baking mix
2 teaspoons ground cinnamon
½ teaspoon ground nutmeg
2 pounds fresh peaches (about
8 medium), sliced
Whipped cream (optional)

Combine oats, sugars, baking mix, cinnamon and nutmeg in large bowl. Stir in peaches; mix until well blended. Transfer to **CROCK-POT**® slow cooker. Cover; cook on LOW 4 to 6 hours. Serve warm with whipped cream, if desired.

Pumpkin-Cranberry Custard

Make 4 to 6 servings

1 can (30 ounces) pumpkin pie filling
1 can (12 ounces) evaporated milk
1 cup dried cranberries
4 eggs, beaten
1 cup crushed or whole gingersnap cookies (optional)
Whipped cream (optional)

Combine pumpkin, evaporated milk, cranberries and eggs in **CROCK-POT**® slow cooker; mix thoroughly. Cover; cook on HIGH 4 to 4½ hours. Serve with crushed or whole gingersnaps and whipped cream, if desired.

Cran-Apple Orange Conserve

Makes about 5 cups

2 medium oranges, washed

5 large tart apples, peeled, cored and chopped

2 cups sugar

1½ cups fresh cranberries

1 tablespoon grated lemon peel

1. Remove thin slice from both ends of both oranges for easier chopping. Finely chop unpeeled oranges (remove any seeds) to yield about 2 cups of chopped oranges.

2. Combine chopped oranges, apples, sugar, cranberries and lemon peel in **CROCK-POT**® slow cooker. Cover; cook on LOW 4 hours or on HIGH 2 hours.

3. Slightly crush fruit with potato masher. Cook, uncovered, on LOW 2 hours or on HIGH 1 to 1½ hours or until very thick, stirring occasionally to prevent sticking. Cool at least 2 hours. Serve over pound cake or with waffles or pancakes.

Tip: *Fruit conserve can also be served with roast pork or poultry.*

Homestyle Apple Brown Betty

Makes 8 servings

6 cups cooking apples, peeled, cored and cut into eighths
1 cup bread crumbs
1 teaspoon ground cinnamon
1 teaspoon ground nutmeg
⅛ teaspoon salt
¾ cup packed light brown sugar
½ cup (1 stick) butter or margarine, melted
¼ cup finely chopped walnuts
  Whipped cream or vanilla ice cream (optional)

1. Coat **CROCK-POT®** slow cooker with nonstick cooking spray. Place apples in bottom.

2. Combine bread crumbs, cinnamon, nutmeg, salt, sugar, butter and walnuts. Spread over apples. Cover; cook on LOW 3 to 4 hours or on HIGH 2 hours. Serve warm with whipped cream, if desired.

Tip: For 5-, 6-, or 7-quart **CROCK-POT®** slow cookers, double all ingredients.

Apple-Date Crisp

Makes 6 servings

6 **cups thinly sliced peeled apples (about 6 medium apples, preferably Golden Delicious)**

2 **teaspoons lemon juice**

⅓ **cup chopped dates**

1⅓ **cups uncooked quick oats**

½ **cup all-purpose flour**

½ **cup packed light brown sugar**

½ **teaspoon ground cinnamon**

¼ **teaspoon ground ginger**

¼ **teaspoon salt**

Dash ground nutmeg

Dash ground cloves (optional)

4 **tablespoons (½ stick) cold butter, cut into small pieces**

1. Coat **CROCK-POT**® slow cooker with nonstick cooking spray. Place apples in medium bowl. Sprinkle with lemon juice; toss to coat. Add dates and mix well. Transfer mixture to **CROCK-POT**® slow cooker.

2. For topping, combine oats, flour, sugar, cinnamon, ginger, salt, nutmeg and cloves, if desired, in medium bowl. Cut in butter with pastry blender or 2 knives until mixture resembles coarse crumbs. Sprinkle oat mixture over apples; smooth top. Cover; cook on LOW about 4 hours or on HIGH about 2 hours, or until apples are tender.

Tip: Simmer a sweet treat in your **CROCK-POT**® slow cooker during dinner, so you can delight your family and guests with an appetizing warm dessert.

Chocolate Croissant Pudding

Makes 6 servings

1½ **cups milk**

3 **eggs**

½ **cup sugar**

¼ **cup unsweetened cocoa powder**

½ **teaspoon vanilla**

¼ **teaspoon salt**

2 **plain croissants, cut into 1-inch pieces, divided**

½ **cup chocolate chips, divided**
 Whipped cream

1. Prepare 1 quart casserole, soufflé dish or other high-sided baking pan that will fit in your **CROCK-POT®** slow cooker by coating with nonstick cooking spray.

2. Beat milk, eggs, sugar, cocoa, vanilla and salt in medium bowl. Layer half of croissants, ¼ cup chocolate chips and half of egg mixture into prepared casserole. Repeat layers with remaining croissants, chocolate chips and egg mixture.

3. Place rack or trivet into **CROCK-POT®** slow cooker; pour in 1 cup water. Place casserole on rack. Cover; cook on LOW 3 to 4 hours.

4. Remove casserole from **CROCK-POT®** slow cooker. Spoon bread pudding into bowls. Top with whipped cream.

Tip: Straight-sided round casserole or soufflé dishes that fit into the **CROCK-POT®** stoneware make excellent baking dishes for breads, cakes, and desserts.

Mixed Berry Cobbler

Makes 8 servings

1	package (16 ounces) frozen mixed berries
¾	cup granulated sugar
2	tablespoons quick-cooking tapioca
2	teaspoons grated lemon peel
1½	cups all-purpose flour
½	cup packed light brown sugar
2¼	teaspoons baking powder
¼	teaspoon ground nutmeg
¾	cup milk
⅓	cup butter, melted
	Vanilla ice cream or whipped cream (optional)

1. Coat **CROCK-POT®** slow cooker with nonstick cooking spray. Stir together berries, granulated sugar, tapioca and lemon peel in medium bowl. Transfer to **CROCK-POT®** slow cooker.

2. For topping, combine flour, brown sugar, baking powder and nutmeg in medium bowl. Add milk and butter; stir just until blended. Drop spoonfuls of dough on top of berry mixture. Cover; cook on LOW 4 hours. Uncover; let stand about 30 minutes. Serve with ice cream, if desired.

Tip: Cobblers are year-round favorites. Experiment with seasonal fresh fruits, such as pears, plums, peaches, rhubarb, blueberries, raspberries, strawberries, blackberries or gooseberries. Try different apple varieties, including newer ones such as Pink Lady, or a blend of your favorite apples to come up with your own signature cobbler.

Baked Ginger Apples

Makes 4 servings

- **4** large Red Delicious apples
- **½** cup (1 stick) unsalted butter, melted
- **⅓** cup chopped macadamia nuts
- **¼** cup chopped dried apricots
- **2** tablespoons finely chopped crystallized ginger
- **1** tablespoon dark brown sugar
- **¾** cup brandy
- **½** cup vanilla pudding and pie filling mix
- **2** cups heavy cream

1. Slice tops off apples; remove cores. Combine butter, nuts, apricots, ginger and brown sugar in medium bowl. Fill apples with nut mixture. Transfer to **CROCK-POT**® slow cooker. Pour brandy over apples. Cover; cook on LOW 4 hours or on HIGH 2 hours.

2. Gently remove apples from **CROCK-POT**® slow cooker with slotted spoon; cover with foil to keep warm.

3. Combine pudding mix and cream in small bowl. Add to cooking liquid in **CROCK-POT**® slow cooker; mix well. Cover; cook on HIGH 30 minutes. Stir until smooth. Return apples to **CROCK-POT**® slow cooker; keep warm until ready to serve with warm cream sauce.

Tip: Don't worry about using spirits or liqueurs in slow-cooked dessert recipes. The gentle heat causes the alcohol content to cook away, leaving only the delicious flavor behind.

Peach Cobbler

Makes 4 to 6 servings

2 packages (16 ounces each) frozen peaches, thawed and drained
¾ cup plus 1 tablespoon sugar, divided
2 teaspoons ground cinnamon, divided
½ teaspoon ground nutmeg
¾ cup all-purpose flour
6 tablespoons butter, cut into small pieces
Whipped cream (optional)

1. Combine peaches, ¾ cup sugar, 1½ teaspoons cinnamon and nutmeg in medium bowl. Transfer to **CROCK-POT®** slow cooker.

2. For topping, combine flour, remaining 1 tablespoon sugar and remaining ½ teaspoon cinnamon in small bowl. Cut in butter with pastry blender or 2 knives until mixture resembles coarse crumbs. Sprinkle over peach mixture. Cover; cook on HIGH 2 hours. Serve with freshly whipped cream, if desired.

Tip: *To make cleanup easier when cooking sticky or sugary foods, spray the inside of the* **CROCK-POT®** *slow cooker with nonstick cooking spray before adding ingredients.*

Fruit Ambrosia with Dumplings

Makes 4 to 6 servings

4 cups fresh or frozen fruit*
½ cup plus 2 tablespoons granulated sugar, divided
½ cup warm apple or cran-apple juice
2 tablespoons quick-cooking tapioca
1 cup all-purpose flour
1¼ teaspoons baking powder
¼ teaspoon salt
3 tablespoons butter or margarine, cut into small pieces
½ cup milk
1 large egg
2 tablespoons light brown sugar, plus additional for garnish
Vanilla ice cream, whipped cream *or* fruity yogurt (optional)

Use strawberries, raspberries, blueberries or peaches.

1. Combine fruit, ½ cup granulated sugar, juice and tapioca in **CROCK-POT**® slow cooker. Cover; cook on LOW 5 to 6 hours or on HIGH 2½ to 3 hours, or until fruit forms thick sauce.

2. Combine flour, 2 tablespoons granulated sugar, baking powder and salt in mixing bowl. Cut in butter using pastry cutter or 2 knives until mixture resembles coarse crumbs. Stir together milk and egg in small bowl. Pour milk and egg mixture into flour mixture. Stir until soft dough forms.

3. Turn **CROCK-POT**® slow cooker to HIGH. Drop dough by teaspoonfuls on top of fruit. Sprinkle dumplings with brown sugar. Cover; cook 30 minutes to 1 hour or until toothpick inserted in dumplings comes out clean.

4. Sprinkle dumplings with additional brown sugar, if desired. Serve warm. Garnish as desired.

Decadent Chocolate Delight

Makes 12 servings

- 1 package (about 18 ounces) chocolate cake mix
- 1 container (8 ounces) sour cream
- 1 cup semisweet chocolate chips
- 1 cup water
- 4 eggs
- ¾ cup vegetable oil
- 1 package (4-serving size) instant chocolate pudding and pie filling mix

Coat **CROCK-POT**® slow cooker with nonstick cooking spray. Combine all ingredients in medium bowl; mix well. Transfer to **CROCK-POT**® slow cooker. Cover; cook on LOW 3 to 4 hours or on HIGH 1½ to 1¾ hours. Serve hot or warm with ice cream.

Triple Chocolate Fantasy

Makes 36 servings

- 2 pounds white almond bark, broken into pieces
- 1 bar (4 ounces) German chocolate, broken into pieces
- 1 package (12 ounces) semi-sweet chocolate chips
- 3 cups lightly toasted, coarsely chopped pecans

1. Place chocolates in **CROCK-POT®** slow cooker. Cover; cook on HIGH 1 hour. Do not stir.

2. Turn **CROCK-POT®** slow cooker to LOW. Continue cooking 1 hour, stirring every 15 minutes. Stir in nuts.

3. Drop mixture by tablespoonfuls onto baking sheet covered with waxed paper; let cool. Store in tightly covered container.

Tip: Make a variety of chocolate candies for gifts or special occasions by substituting these mix-ins for the pecans: raisins, peanuts or pistachios candied cherries, crushed toffee, toasted coconut, miniature marshmallows or crushed peppermints.

Cherry Delight

Makes 8 to 10 servings

1 can (21 ounces) cherry pie filling
1 package (18¼ ounces) yellow cake mix
½ cup (1 stick) butter, melted
⅓ cup chopped walnuts
   Whipped topping or vanilla ice cream (optional)

Place pie filling in **CROCK-POT**® slow cooker. Mix together cake mix and butter in medium bowl. Spread evenly over cherry filling. Sprinkle walnuts on top. Cover; cook on LOW 3 to 4 hours or HIGH 1½ to 2 hours. Spoon into serving dishes, and serve warm with whipped topping or ice cream, if desired.

Cherry Flan

Makes 6 servings

5 eggs
½ cup sugar
½ teaspoon salt
¾ cup all-purpose flour
1 can (12 ounces) evaporated milk
1 teaspoon vanilla
1 bag (16 ounces) frozen pitted dark sweet cherries, thawed
   Whipped cream or cherry vanilla ice cream

1. Coat **CROCK-POT**® slow cooker with nonstick cooking spray. Beat eggs, sugar and salt in large bowl with electric mixer at high speed until thick and pale yellow. Add flour; beat until smooth. Beat in evaporated milk and vanilla.

2. Pour batter into prepared **CROCK-POT**® slow cooker. Place cherries evenly over batter. Cover; cook on LOW 3½ to 4 hours or until flan is set. Serve warm with whipped cream.

Cherry Delight

Fresh Berry Compote

Makes 4 servings

- **2 cups fresh blueberries**
- **4 cups fresh sliced strawberries**
- **2 tablespoons orange juice**
- **½ to ¾ cup sugar**
- **4 slices (½ inch×1½ inches) lemon peel with no white pith**
- **1 cinnamon stick *or* ½ teaspoon ground cinnamon**

1. Place blueberries in **CROCK-POT**® slow cooker. Cover; cook on HIGH 45 minutes, until blueberries begin to soften.

2. Add strawberries, orange juice, ½ cup sugar, lemon peel and cinnamon stick. Stir to blend. Cover; cook 1 to 1½ hours, or until berries soften and sugar dissolves. Check for sweetness and add more sugar if necessary, cooking until added sugar dissolves.

3. Transfer **CROCK-POT**® stoneware insert from heating unit to heatproof surface to cool. Serve compote warm or chilled.

Tip: *To turn this compote into a fresh-fruit topping for cake, ice cream, waffles or pancakes, carefully spoon out fruit, leaving cooking liquid in* **CROCK-POT**® *slow cooker. Blend 1 to 2 tablespoons cornstarch with ¼ cup cold water until smooth. Add to cooking liquid and cook on HIGH until thickened. Return fruit to sauce and blend in gently.*

Strawberry Rhubarb Crisp

Makes 8 servings

Fruit

4	cups sliced hulled strawberries
4	cups diced rhubarb (about 5 stalks), cut into ½-inch dice
1½	cups granulated sugar
2	tablespoons lemon juice
1½	tablespoons cornstarch, plus water (optional)

Topping

1	cup all-purpose flour
1	cup old-fashioned oats
½	cup granulated sugar
½	cup brown sugar
½	teaspoon ground ginger
½	teaspoon ground nutmeg
½	cup butter (1 stick), cut into pieces
½	cup sliced almonds, toasted*

To toast almonds, spread in single layer on baking sheet. Bake in preheated 350°F oven 8 to 10 minutes or until golden brown, stirring frequently.

1. Prepare fruit. Coat **CROCK-POT**® slow cooker with nonstick cooking spray. Place strawberries, rhubarb, granulated sugar and lemon juice in **CROCK-POT**® slow cooker and mix well. Cook on HIGH 1½ hours or until fruit is tender.

2. If fruit is dry after cooking, add a little water. If fruit has too much liquid, mix cornstarch with a small amount of water and stir into fruit. Cook on HIGH an additional 15 minutes or until cooking liquid is thickened.

3. Preheat oven to 375°F. Prepare topping. Combine flour, oats, sugars, ginger and nutmeg in medium bowl. Cut in butter using pastry cutter or 2 knives until mixture resembles coarse crumbs. Stir in almonds.

4. Remove lid from **CROCK-POT**® slow cooker and gently sprinkle topping onto fruit. Transfer stoneware to oven. Bake 15 to 20 minutes or until topping begins to brown.

Spiced Plums and Pears

Makes 6 to 8 servings

2   cans (29 ounces each) sliced pears in heavy syrup, undrained
2   pounds black or red plums (about 12 to 14), pitted and sliced
1   cup packed light brown sugar
1   teaspoon ground cinnamon
½   teaspoon ground ginger
¼   teaspoon grated lemon peel
2   tablespoons cornstarch
2   tablespoons water
     Pound cake or ice cream
     Whipped topping

1. Cut pear slices in half with spoon. Place pears, plums, sugar, cinnamon, ginger and lemon peel in **CROCK-POT®** slow cooker. Cover; cook on HIGH 4 hours.

2. Combine cornstarch and water to make smooth paste. Stir into fruit mixture. Cook on HIGH until slightly thickened.

3. Serve warm or at room temperature over pound cake with whipped topping.

*Tip: When adapting conventionally prepared recipes for your **CROCK-POT®** slow cooker, revise the amount of spices you use. For example, whole spices increase in flavor while ground spices tend to lose flavor during slow cooking. If you prefer, you can adjust the seasonings or add spices just before serving the dish.*

Sublime
Sipping

Slow cooking yields subtle flavors

Mulled Cranberry Tea

Makes 8 servings

- **2 tea bags**
- **1 cup boiling water**
- **1 bottle (48 ounces) cranberry juice**
- **½ cup dried cranberries (optional)**
- **⅓ cup sugar**
- **1 large lemon, cut into ¼-inch slices**
- **4 cinnamon sticks**
- **6 whole cloves**
- **Additional thin lemon slices and cinnamon sticks (optional)**

1. Place tea bags in **CROCK-POT**® slow cooker. Pour boiling water over tea bags; cover and let steep 5 minutes. Remove and discard tea bags.

2. Stir in cranberry juice, cranberries, if desired, sugar, lemon slices, 4 cinnamon sticks and cloves. Cover; cook on LOW 2 to 3 hours or on HIGH 1 to 2 hours.

3. Remove and discard cooked lemon slices, cinnamon sticks and cloves. Serve in warm mug with fresh lemon slice and cinnamon stick, if desired.

*Tip: The flavor and aroma of crushed or ground herbs and spices may lessen during a longer cooking time. So, for slow cooking in your **CROCK-POT**® slow cooker, you may use whole herbs and spices. Be sure to taste and adjust your seasonings before serving.*

Spiced Citrus Tea

Makes 6 servings

4 tea bags
   Peel of 1 orange
4 cups boiling water
3 tablespoons honey
2 cans (6 ounces each) orange-pineapple juice
3 star anise
3 cinnamon sticks
   Strawberries, raspberries or kiwis (optional)

Place tea bags, orange peel and water in **CROCK-POT**® slow cooker; cover and let steep 10 minutes. Remove and discard tea bags and orange peel. Add remaining ingredients; cover; cook on LOW 3 hours. Garnish as desired.

Chai Tea

Makes 8 to 10 servings

- 2 **quarts (8 cups) water**
- 8 **bags black tea**
- ¾ **cup sugar***
- 16 **whole cloves**
- 16 **whole cardamom seeds, pods removed (optional)**
- 5 **cinnamon sticks**
- 8 **slices fresh ginger**
- 1 **cup milk**

Chai tea is typically sweet. For less-sweet tea, reduce sugar to ½ cup.

1. Combine water, tea, sugar, cloves, cardamom, if desired, cinnamon and ginger in slow cooker. Cover; cook on HIGH 2 to 2½ hours.

2. Strain mixture; discard solids. (At this point, tea may be covered and refrigerated up to 3 days.)

3. Stir in milk just before serving. Serve warm or chilled.

Warm and Spicy Fruit Punch

Makes about 14 servings

4   cinnamon sticks
1   orange, washed
1   square (8 inches) double-thickness cheesecloth
1   teaspoon whole allspice
½   teaspoon whole cloves
7   cups water
1   can (12 ounces) frozen cran-raspberry juice concentrate, thawed
1   can (6 ounces) frozen lemonade concentrate, thawed
2   cans (5½ ounces each) apricot nectar

1. Break cinnamon into pieces. Using vegetable peeler, remove strips of orange peel. Squeeze juice from orange; set juice aside.

2. Rinse cheesecloth; squeeze out water. Wrap cinnamon, orange peel, allspice and cloves in cheesecloth. Tie bag securely with cotton string or strip of cheesecloth.

3. Combine reserved orange juice, water, concentrates and apricot nectar in **CROCK-POT**® slow cooker; add spice bag. Cover; cook on LOW 5 to 6 hours. Remove and discard spice bag before serving.

Tip: *To keep punch warm during a party, place your* **CROCK-POT**® *slow cooker on the buffet table, and turn the setting to LOW or WARM.*

Triple Delicious Hot Chocolate

Makes 6 servings

- ⅓ **cup sugar**
- ¼ **cup unsweetened cocoa powder**
- ¼ **teaspoon salt**
- 3 **cups milk, divided**
- ¾ **teaspoon vanilla**
- 1 **cup heavy cream**
- 1 **square (1 ounce) bittersweet chocolate**
- 1 **square (1 ounce) white chocolate**
- ¾ **cup whipped cream**
- 6 **teaspoons mini chocolate chips or shaved bittersweet chocolate**

1. Combine sugar, cocoa, salt and ½ cup milk in medium bowl. Beat until smooth. Transfer to **CROCK-POT**® slow cooker. Add remaining 2½ cups milk and vanilla; stir in. Cover; cook on LOW 2 hours.

2. Add cream. Cover; cook on LOW 10 minutes. Stir in bittersweet and white chocolates until melted.

3. Pour hot chocolate into 6 coffee cups. Top each serving with 2 tablespoons whipped cream and 1 teaspoon chocolate chips.

Mulled Apple Cider

Makes 10 servings

2	quarts bottled apple cider or juice (not unfiltered)
¼	cup packed light brown sugar
1	square (8 inches) double-thickness cheesecloth
8	allspice berries
4	cinnamon sticks, broken into halves
12	whole cloves
1	large orange
	Additional cinnamon sticks (optional)

1. Combine apple cider and brown sugar in **CROCK-POT**® slow cooker.

2. Rinse cheesecloth; squeeze out water. Wrap allspice berries and cinnamon stick halves in cheesecloth; tie securely with cotton string or strip of cheesecloth.

3. Stick cloves randomly into orange; cut orange into quarters. Place spice bag and orange quarters in cider mixture. Cover; cook on HIGH 2½ to 3 hours.

4. Once cooked, **CROCK-POT**® slow cooker may be turned to LOW to keep cider warm up to 3 additional hours. Remove and discard spice bag and orange before serving. Ladle cider into mugs. Garnish with additional cinnamon sticks, if desired.

Tip: To make inserting cloves into the orange a little easier, first pierce the orange skin with the point of wooden skewer. Remove the skewer and insert a clove.

Index

Index

Index

Index

Index

Index

Index

Notes